ZUNI FETISHES

ZUNI FETISHES

USING NATIVE AMERICAN OBJECTS
FOR MEDITATION, REFLECTION, AND INSIGHT

HAL ZINA BENNETT, PH.D.

HarperSanFrancisco
A Division of HarperCollins*Publishers*

Harper San Francisco and the author, in association with the Rainforest Action Network, will facilitate the planting of two trees for every one tree used in the manufacture of this book.

Through arrangements with the publisher, ten percent of the author's earnings on this book, beyond the original advance, are donated to: **Habitat for Humanity International,** 121 Habitat Street, P.O. Box 6439, Americus, GA 31709-6439, to help continue the mission of providing simple homes so that everyone can have a decent place to live.

Library of Congress Cataloging-in-Publication Data
Bennett, Hal Zina
Zuni fetishes : using Native American objects for meditation, reflection, and insight / Hal Zina Bennett.
p. cm.
Includes bibliographical references.
ISBN 0–06–250069–4 (acid-free paper)
1. Zuni Indians—Religion and mythology.   2. Fetishes (Ceremonial objects)—New Mexico.   3. Zuni Indians—Rites and ceremonies.   I. Title.
E99.Z9B45 1993

299'.75—dc20

92–53210
CIP

94 95 96 97 ❖ RRD(H) 11 10 9 8 7 6

This edition is printed on acid-free paper that meets the American National Standards Institute Z39.48 Standard.

*This book is dedicated to my teacher,
Awahakeewah, Master Toolmaker, whose wisdom about the use of the
Creative Spirit in all of us has taught me to respect, honor, and love the gifts
bestowed upon us by a power much greater than ourselves.*

CONTENTS

ACKNOWLEDGMENTS

Each time I write a book I am reminded that publishing is a complex collaborative process, involving editors, book designers, copyeditors, editorial assistants—the list goes on and on. These are the behind-the-scenes heroes and heroines who put in long hours, hoping to make every book they touch a success. It is not possible to produce a book without them, yet we seldom see their names mentioned in the books they bring to the reading public. I would like to thank every one of them.

My thanks go first to Hilary Vartanian, my editor on this project. Her enthusiasm has inspired me exactly at those times when I most needed a creative jump-start, and her professionalism in guiding the book through its various stages has made the entire process effortless for me.

To Timothy White, who provided the illustrations for the fetishes, I would like to extend special gratitude. We have been friends for seven years now, and as the publisher of the magazine *Shaman's Drum*, he has been a continuous source of wisdom, inspiration, and support not only for me but for the cause of all Native Americans. His drawings here, like his magazine, help to provide a bridge between worlds.

▲▲ ACKNOWLEDGMENTS ▲▲

Thanks to all the people at Harper San Francisco—Tom Grady, Michael Toms, Mark Salzwedel, Robin Seaman, Mimi Kusch, Dean Burrell, Jamie Sue Brooks, and the many others whom I have never met.

For the wonderful cover design, thanks to Kathy Warinner. And many thanks to Nancy Palmer Jones, my copyeditor.

There are two people whose assistance and friendship have been especially appreciated—Tony Barnett and Don Sharp. Their knowledge of fetishes, Native American crafts, and the modern Zuni community has been most helpful.

Thanks, also, to my friends in Zuni who continue to provide spiritual direction and inspiration for people the world over.

Last and certainly not least, I would like to thank my family, particularly my wife, Susan Sparrow, who puts up with my eccentricities and apparently has learned to love them. Thanks, too, to my son Nathan Bennett, who took time out between his professional shoots to provide the photo of the Bear fetish that inspired the cover art and the author's photograph for the jacket of this book.

Thank you one and all!

I BECAME INTERESTED IN ZUNI FETISHES twenty years ago, in the early 1970s. Most of the literature on them that I initially found was of two kinds: first, books written for collectors of Native American artifacts, which identified fetishes according to region of origin and listed their monetary value to collectors; second, brief and only occasional mention of fetishes in anthropology and archaeology texts, which as often as not wrongly described them as "objects of superstition." While I found these references only mildly interesting, they did help me to recognize the important role fetishes played in the daily lives of a society that was both humble and highly evolved. I began to realize that the fetishes, like symbols that could be held in the hand, expressed values and beliefs that had guided people's decisions in their pursuit of physical, mental, and spiritual well-being.

In my search for a deeper understanding of the Zunis' use of fetishes, I came upon the writings of Frank Hamilton Cushing. Born in 1857, this remarkable man was able to provide a cultural bridge between the European and the Native American minds. Much more than an intellectual who stood outside his subject and studied it as a biologist might study a butterfly skewered on a pin, Cushing immersed himself in the daily life of the Zuni. His own biography suggests that he must have been put on the earth for the purpose of providing that cultural bridge for which his extraordinary early life prepared him.

In her introduction to Cushing's *Zuni Folk Tales*,[1] Mary Austen described him as being "of that physical constitution which a few hundred years earlier gave rise to the belief in changelings, so small and frail at birth that he spent his first three years on a pillow, and so phenomenally gifted that he seems to have remembered practically everything that happened to him from his first year."

Owing to his frail stature, he was exempt from school. The young Cushing spent his time in the woods, developing an extraordinary affinity with wildlife, even inventing a language for himself and the creatures of the forest. He also developed a strong interest in the vanished Native American peoples of the Lake Erie region, uncovering artifacts and reconstructing lost techniques of these societies that had stumped even the best archaeologists. At the age of nine, he began to collect arrowheads, along with explanations about their use and how they were formed; these would later become part of the Smithsonian Institution's permanent collection.

In 1879, when Cushing was only twenty-two, he was asked to accompany the famous explorer of the American West, Major John Wesley Powell, on an expedition to what is now Zuni, New Mexico, a region that was then entirely unexplored. Cushing was to be a field collector for the Bureau of American Ethnology. The purpose of this mission was to collect information on the Native Americans for the Smithsonian Institution's permanent records.

At his own request, Cushing was left at the Zuni pueblo, where he would spend the next six years of his life. After mastering the Zuni language—perhaps the only person of European stock ever to do so—he was adopted into the Macaw clan and given the sacred name of Medicine-flower. He so faithfully applied himself to studying and meeting the tribal requirements that he became Priest of the Bow, living with the Zuni governor's family and exercising important religious duties in the pueblo.

During his lifetime, Cushing recorded many of the myths and legends of the Zuni people. For me one of his most exciting works was his study of the Zuni fetish, in which he revealed how the various figures—such as Bear, Mountain Lion, Badger, Eagle, and Mole—fit into the Zunis' cosmology and spiritual belief systems.

Cushing's notes, as well as the notes of those who knew and worked with him, provide evidence that his interest in Native American ways, particularly in their metaphysical and spiritual beliefs, was sparked by a strong sense of personal mission. According to Mary Austen, there was always present in the back of Cushing's mind a belief that there existed "a Sacred Myth, involving a cosmogony, a Creator, a company of Surpassing Beings, and profoundly mystical prototypes for every essential motion of man's soul."[2] He made an outline, with partial translations of this epic Creation Myth, but it was never finished, owing to his untimely death in 1900.

Cushing's study of Zuni fetishes and the complex and sophisticated society from which they come is a rare and valuable achievement. He was able to record and retain for all those who might follow a relatively accurate, although partial, picture of traditions that are fast disappearing from the earth. His special gifts allowed him to immerse himself in the Zuni culture so that he all but became one of them. Mary Austen says of him, "Perhaps he was, in fact, a changeling, a throw-back to the mysterious little people, traces of whose life, so close to the earth, make a network of fairy lore over ancestral Europe. He remains uniquely the only man not of their blood who understood."[3]

Throughout this book, I refer to Cushing's work again and again, for it was his influence that prompted me to treat fetishism not as an archaic, superstitious practice of "prescientific" societies but as a practice with valuable applications for modern life.

WHERE TECHNOLOGY AND ANCIENT
INTUITIVE TRADITIONS MEET

Even as our lives have become more and more technologized, we have also become increasingly interested in exploring the intuitive wisdom of ancient cultures. We are beginning to recognize that we have much to learn from these early civilizations and that our very survival may depend on their wisdom. They have much to teach us about living in harmony with nature, appreciating that everything on this planet is an essential part of an intricate web that we must love and protect.

In recent years, partially as a result of explorations at the outer edges of modern science, we have come full circle, from viewing the universe as a gigantic machine all of whose rules of operation we would eventually discover and harness for our own use, to perceiving the universe as a "thought." There is a kind of poetic irony in this, that science would rebut the vision that initiated it and ask us once again to search for answers to the puzzle of human life and the cosmos through the great spiritual disciplines of the world. And not the least of these disciplines is Native American spirituality.

In our search for values to guide our lives, we have found that one of the most fruitful regions to explore is the "inner world," that region sometimes described as the "invisible reality" that influences our lives. This is the world of dream, imagination, and spirituality. Of course, this is not a new development; even in the European traditions as far back as Aristotle, there was the argument that the route to understanding the external world would be found by first understanding the nature and limits of the observer.

For most Westerners, the first thing that comes to mind when we speak of the inner world is Sigmund Freud, who imagined that the causes of "man's cruelty to man," as the poet Marianne Moore once said, could be found in material stored in the unconscious. While he may have provided one piece of the puzzle, Freud never succeeded in identifying or helping people get in touch with the life-affirming drives that seem to form an invisible bond between all peoples. It is this latter that ultimately provides us with the positive guidance that we seek in intuitive, religious, and spiritual disciplines, rather than psychological systems. It is in this search for our life-affirming essence that I have found the Zuni fetishes so helpful.

In my treatment of the Zuni fetish that you'll find in the pages ahead, the point of view is decidedly in favor of the fact that these artifacts, still produced in Zuni, New Mexico, today, along with the techniques that are allied with them, can serve us in modern life. However, I would like it to be noted that I claim no authority in, nor do I advocate all the practices and beliefs of the ancient Zuni theology per se. What I do advocate is that in our search for values, in modern life as in the past, we explore the wisdom of as many social and spiritual disciplines as we can.

Like Cushing I am an outsider where the genuine life of the Zuni is concerned. I do not have the long bloodline, and do not share in that collective unconscious that even today continues to shape the hearts and minds of these peoples. My only claim is that I have gone to them to learn, to share some of the wisdom that perhaps can bring us closer to those invisible bonds which make us One.

If the use of Zuni fetishes can serve the reader in her or his own quest for a better life, so much the better for us all. Not all readers, of course, will find them helpful in this way, and that's alright, too. One may be attracted to them as a collector, or out of being in some way artistically moved by them. I would hope that this book might enrich whatever interest you bring to this subject, shining one small light onto an ancient theme much greater than any single one of us.

INTRODUCTION

JUMPING THE CHASM

As you go forward into your life, you will come upon a great chasm.
Jump. It is not as wide as you think.

—ADVICE TO A YOUNG NATIVE AMERICAN
UPON INITIATION INTO ADULTHOOD[1]

IN THE SOUTHWEST, where they still live, Zunis are respected and sought out by other peoples in the area for their artistry in making fetishes.* In the past twenty years their reputation has spread worldwide. What is especially intriguing about the Zuni fetish is its simple yet evocative quality. It is almost impossible to see one or to hold one in your hand without sensing its importance. The best fetishes evoke in our minds countless images of the animal they portray—images of the animal as we have seen it in real life or as we have imagined it from what we have read in books or observed in movies.

The Zunis are by no means the only people who have used fetishes. Most early societies had power figures of various kinds, small personal artifacts that could usually be held in the hand and

---

* The Zuni homeland is located in New Mexico, west of Albuquerque and twenty miles east of the Arizona border.

that were believed to confer power to their owner. Usually the power figures were shaped from materials common to the area where their maker lived. They have been found carved of wood or shaped out of bronze, stone, or even a precious metal such as gold.

These figures were believed to derive their power from various sources, depending on the cosmology or religious beliefs of the people who made and possessed them. Some were believed to be gods, requiring constant attention and rewarding the faithful with special favors. Others, like talismans, were believed to possess powers to protect their owners against certain dangers. Still others, like the totems of the indigenous peoples of the Northwest, were believed to represent ancestral lineages, offering power and guidance by reminding the people of their loyalties to past generations.

While the use of fetishes is not unique to the Zuni, their particular application of them probably is. Originally, these figures were tools of the hunter. Prior to a hunt, a man (women rarely hunted) might sit before several figures—that is, fetishes—and ask them for help in the task ahead. Through them, he believed he could communicate with the spirit either of the game he was hunting (for example, elk or deer) or of the master hunter (the mountain lion). The hunter might pray to the spirit of the animal asking its permission to be killed in order to benefit the tribe. He might also ask the master hunter, Mountain Lion, for help with tracking his prey.

By focusing on the fetish, the hunter could feel and see in his mind's eye and in his heart the living presence of the animal—how it moved, the sounds it made, its smell, its hunting and mating habits, and its treatment of its young. All this was not just raw information that was confined to the head the way an accountant might look at a column of figures or a computer programmer at a set of commands. With the help of the fetish, the hunter evoked for himself complex sensory data—smells, sights, touch, feelings—that have an instinctual power far beyond that of more linear information.

While the most commonly recognized use of Zuni fetishes is this application to the hunt, they were also used in healing everything from a couple's infertility to a drought affecting an entire area. Thus, they could represent for the Zunis important spiritual and religious beliefs. Like the icons of the Christian faith, the fetishes had a symbolic intent and were used to remind a person of the values that might help him or her live a more harmonious and reverent life.

As we learn about a particular fetish, growing increasingly sensitive to such factors as who made it, the material from which it was shaped, which animal it depicts, how it fits into the sophisticated society from which it emerged, and what lessons it has to teach us, the fetish's own story begins to emerge. We develop a particular emotional or spiritual relationship to the object, just as we do with a work of art or a piece of music that deeply moves us. And just as with the work of art or piece of music, we may feel pleasantly uplifted— happier, more hopeful, more courageous, more loving—from our contact with it. At those times when we feel defeated, the object may remind us of our strengths. At those times when we are having difficulty making a decision, we may be reminded of personal values that will help guide us. At those times when we are feeling lonely and unloved, we can be reminded of our connection with a power greater than ourselves.

We are drawn to these fetishes for many reasons. We may be drawn to them aesthetically, because they are works of art. We may be drawn to them because of an interest in societies other than our own. We may be drawn to them because we experience some connection with the ancient intuitive traditions from which they have sprung, seeing in them a way to access levels of experience from which most of us have become distanced by our fast-paced, technologized way of life. They may remind us of values as important for our survival now as they were in ancient times, such as our connection with the earth and the immutable natural order. Few would argue, in fact, that the Zuni fetish has a special charisma whose allure crosses nearly all cultural boundaries. To discover the source of this charisma, we must turn to the shamanic tradition from which these enchanting figures come.

FETISHES AND THE SHAMANIC TRADITION

There is no simple definition of shamanism, but it can be described as *the quest for wisdom about the intrinsic laws that govern all of life.*

In most indigenous societies, shamans were people who served as teachers, priests, and healers. They dedicated their lives to the study of the "unseen realities" that rule our lives and to understanding how these unseen realities might better serve the people. The shamans were generally held in high esteem by the community, performing roles that in modern life we might assign to doctors, lawyers, psychotherapists, ministers, scientists, or other professionals.

In Frank Hamilton Cushing's writings, he called the Zuni shamans "priests." For example, there was the priest who looked after certain sacred fetishes that belonged to the tribe, fetishes that were very old and had been passed down through many generations. The same priest handled the "finishing" or decorating of new fetishes owned by individuals; this finishing included praying, blessing, cleansing, carving, and sometimes painting.[*]

One of the fetish priest's greatest responsibilities was to conduct the annual three-day ceremony in which the people offered prayers of gratitude to their fetishes.

Similarly, there were shamans, or priests, who worked with the fetishes in order to effect various kinds of change in the community. Such changes might be focused on a new season, a drought, a birth, an illness, a death, the education of a young hunter, a marriage, or any number of other events in which an old order was being replaced by a new one. Priests of the hunt also worked with the fetishes prior to handing them over to the hunters. These priests' efforts helped identify hunting trails. They also called forth the powers of the master hunter, and made the first preliminary efforts to communicate with the spirit of the hunters' prey.

---

[*] Rarely are painted fetishes created today, but some of the ancient ones are still in the possession of Zuni elders and in the collection at the Smithsonian Institution in Washington, D.C.

All of this shamanic activity is based on the Zuni belief that there is an invisible force behind every cycle and phase of life that brings about change. This force might be expressed in new life itself, as in the case of a new baby being born or of the first sprouts of corn appearing after the planting of a new crop. Or it might show up in the form of an imbalance in the body, causing a physical or mental illness. It could take the form of love or perhaps of grief over the death of a loved one, or it could be found in courage, or the lack of it, for a hunter or warrior. The shamans and other members of the tribe gathered wisdom about this invisible force from various sources: tradition, storytelling, communication with the fetishes, observation of nature, insights that followed the offering of a prayer, and other intuitive means such as the visions induced by drumming, dancing, or other sacred practices.

Today, the people who gather wisdom about invisible forces may be physicists, who study matter and energy; psychologists, who study how emotions affect behavior; ecologists, who study the effects of human actions on the environment; meteorologists, who study the weather; or ministers or priests, who study the truths and eternal verities that affect the human soul.

Having spent their lives seeking wisdom of these unseen forces, the shamans or priests were believed to be the most qualified community members to offer prayers, rituals, or other practices to help these changes along. Sometimes the shamans' instructed others in the use of fetishes, which were believed to provide bridges to the unseen reality. Often they told stories related to the fetishes and the animals they represented, stories that were more mythical than real, with animal characters whose misadventures offered allegorical principles (frequently with great humor) that made the ancient wisdom of the fetishes more accessible to all.

MAKING CONTACT WITH UNSEEN REALITIES

In most indigenous societies, from ancient to modern times, the education of the shaman begins with a near-death experience or with an intense personal trial in which the person confronts his or her mortality and the limits of his or her personal knowledge. Once faced with their mortality, the new shamans catch a glimpse of a greater truth. For example, a person might have a vision of the many generations that have preceded him or her and the many more that will follow; from this the shaman might begin to understand the importance of living in peace or of honoring the earth and living in harmony with nature. Or the shaman might become acutely aware of how the unseen realities, such as love and hate, joy and grief, selfishness and a sense of unity with others, continue eternally, while individuals and their personal biases die and are born many times over.

Most of us catch fleeting glimpses of these unseen realities from time to time throughout our lives, convincing us that there is more going on than we usually perceive in our daily lives. Sometimes these glimpses are so fleeting that we barely have time to acknowledge them. At other times they are more prolonged, allowing us to reflect on them and be deeply influenced by them.

In religious literature, these glimpses of another reality are often described as "ecstatic" or "transcendent" moments, while in modern consciousness research they are referred to as "breakthrough experiences." The more we can understand these experiences, whether or not we have experienced them directly, the more profoundly will we understand the fetish and its uses. In fact, the fetishes themselves can help us to experience such transcendent moments.

Perhaps describing my own experiences will be the best way for me to convey an appreciation for these encounters with the unseen reality. They began when, at age sixteen, I contracted a disease called tuloremia, or "rabbit fever," which I got while skinning a sick rabbit that I had shot in a corn field near my home in rural Michigan. Following a few days of flulike symptoms, my fever climbed to 106 degrees, at which point the doctor was called and I was rushed to the hospital. Within hours I had slipped into a coma.

While others may have seen me as having completely withdrawn from awareness, this was not my experience at all. The coma carried me into a world where time and space seemed to vanish; it was a dreamlike existence in which people, places, and situations shifted as quickly as thoughts. In my own mind, I had a profound sense of being at a crossroads, a turning point, somewhere between death and life and somewhere between two realities, one of which I knew nothing about. It was as if I could look down two roads, one to my left, one to my right. The one to my left was dark, unknown, hidden. The one to my right was a long tunnel of light that reminded me of looking into the eye of a tornado, though there was nothing foreboding or dangerous about it.

While in this coma, I saw that what we experience in our daily lives is much more the product of our own minds than it is a reflection of what's "out there." I found this revelation confusing and sensed that if I was to understand anything about life, I would first have to understand this. Thus, I may have had a glimpse into the mysteries of life, but I had also been presented with a puzzle that would hold me hostage for many years.

Months after my recovery from tuloremia, I was again out hunting with a friend, about a hundred miles from my home. I was sitting in the snow with my back against a tree trunk. I felt what I believed to be a rock under me, but when I reached down to retrieve it, it turned out to be a beautifully shaped tomahawk head, its edge still sharp and smooth in spite of having lain half buried for at least a hundred years. Though I didn't know it at the time, this artifact would introduce me to the use of found objects as fetishes.

I still have the tomahawk head today; I keep it among my personal collection of fetishes. I often take it in my hand and run my fingers over the smooth, sculpted surfaces. The first time I did this, I found that I could imagine the toolmaker at work, shaping this object from a large piece of granite. I became awed by the craftsman's skill and was touched by his obvious love of his craft, still evidenced in the smooth, graceful curves. I was deeply moved any time I held this artifact in my hand and thought about the craftsman who had shaped it. In a way I did not yet understand, this experience seemed to carry me into that other reality I had encountered during my near-death experience.

In the 1960s, a few years after these events, I moved to the West Coast. Shortly thereafter I met, by sheer chance, two different shamans, the first one in San Francisco, the second in a little town near Acapulco, Mexico, where I had gone for a summer vacation. Both taught me much about the other reality I was experiencing. The most significant breakthrough came for me during my visit to Mexico.

MOVING BEYOND HUMAN PERCEPTION

The shaman in Mexico took me on a vision quest to a mountaintop. It was here that I encountered—in my mind's eye—a glowing, saucer-shaped object that turned slowly before me. It was a lens, like the lens of a camera, but rather than being made of glass, this lens was a living cell, translucent and soft.

Within the lens I saw images from my childhood—my brothers, the house where I lived, my parents. I saw the fields, streams, and lakes where I had spent so much time as a boy. The lens turned in the air. For a long time I just sat quietly and watched. Inside it was an ethereal world, made up of all the experiences of my life. I thought about how people saw their lives flash before their eyes. Was I near death again? It didn't seem likely, yet this vision vividly reawakened the near-death experience of my youth.

By the time the vision was over, I had begun to understand its meaning. The lens represented human perception, the mental facility we all have that allows us to make sense of the world. And it revealed to me that although this facility allows us to get along in the physical world, it also distorts and hides from us other realities than those we can literally see, particularly those that we have defined as "spiritual."

Perhaps one of the most comforting aspects of this vision was the realization that we each have our own lens, our own emotional truths and interpretations of reality. If there are bridges between our minds, they are surely to be found in the spiritual realm, where we recognize links between ourselves and others and between ourselves and the earth that transcend the reality perceived through our own lens.

Back home in San Francisco, I returned to college, where I began to study modern consciousness research and shamanism. The consciousness researchers had much to say about how we create our perceptions of the world in our own minds. This intrigued me as much as did my study of shamanism, where I found references to ancient texts in which the equivalent of our lens of perception was described as a gift from our Creator. Each of these gifts is absolutely essential for creating a *whole* that no single one of us is fully able to grasp. At any given moment, that whole would be incomplete if we excluded even a single lens that is now, ever was, or ever will be in existence.

For me, the most exciting discovery in all this is the realization that when the lens and all it contains are embraced and when they are integrated with the greater spiritual vision, we gain a source of guidance and an ability to express ourselves that is the highest manifestation of our being. In other words, when we join our individual vision of life with the eternal and express this new vision through our work and our relationships, then we simultaneously give and receive the greatest gift of all, which is to come into oneness with our universal identity.

One day, soon after this realization, I picked up the tomahawk head as I had done many times before. This time, however, I felt that it was possible for me not only to imagine its maker* but to communicate with him. Were the subsequent dialogues I had with the tomahawk's maker "real"? Were they taking place only in my imagination? Or were they, through the lens of perception, somehow connecting me with another reality? These were questions I could not answer, yet they motivated me to seek further.

---

* The craftsman who appeared to me has become as real to me as any character in a novel or a movie. Several years ago, he told me he was called Awahakeewah, a name by which I have addressed him ever since.

FURTHER EDUCATION IN THE USE OF FETISHES

Many years after I first received the tomahawk head, a friend who had noticed it on my desk gave me a small stone figure of a bear, crudely carved in soft, gray shale. It measures about two inches high by three inches long. It has a bulbous body, a disproportionately small head and tiny turquoise beads for eyes. Attached to its back with a few strands of monofilament fish line are two feathers, one yellow, the other blue, along with a small, carefully carved, and very sharp arrowhead.

I named this fetish "Spirit Bear," and when I began working with it in the way I had learned to do with the tomahawk head, I found myself acutely focused on a particular set of human abilities and qualities. Among them was the ability to stand outside events without judging them, to consider them calmly, with no vested interest in the outcome. In science and psychology, we call this *objectivity* or *positive detachment*; in many spiritual disciplines, it is known as *unconditional love*. This point of view has released me from more moments of conflict and confusion, caused by inner turmoil that I create for myself, than I care to recall. It has also given me courage and renewed insight when I have felt blocked in my writing.[*]

What first impressed me about Spirit Bear was that whenever I put it before me and asked myself questions that were troubling me, I would feel calmer and better in touch with the thoughts and feelings that were truly important to me. I found that like a close and trusted friend, who also was not willing to put up with my moments of petulance, Spirit Bear helped remind me of how it felt to be objective or to come to a problem with unconditional love. It was almost as if he helped me access past experiences that made that objectivity and love more tangible, putting theory into a context that was rooted in my own memories and that therefore made it both more believable and more accessible to me.

---

[*] I hasten to add that my personal interpretation of this fetish does not necessarily conform to Zuni spiritual beliefs.

After nearly two and a half decades of working with Spirit Bear, I find he is useful at those times in my life when my attachment to my own fear, anger, worry, or confusion is blinding me. The fetish is a reminder that there are higher forces in this world than my own selfish interests or ego-bound desires. It helps me focus on those capacities for objectivity and unconditional love that are so difficult to make use of at moments when we most need them. It is not that the fetish itself has power, but when I place it before me, it reminds me to take another look, to shift my perception and seek new answers beyond the obvious.

EXPANDING OUR KNOWLEDGE THROUGH ANCIENT CONSCIOUSNESS TOOLS

Over the years, I have acquired many new fetishes. I have more than a dozen now, each one depicting a particular set of human qualities or phenomena in nature. In my work as a writer, I often request their assistance as I try to get in touch with knowledge that is not otherwise immediately available. In my personal life, the fetishes remind me of the more universal themes that thread their way through the joys, sorrows, victories, and defeats of everyday living.

As we explore in this book the invaluable tools offered us by ancient cultures, I feel it is important to recognize that we do so not because they are superior to the logical, scientific, and more obviously structured left-brain tools we have developed over the past few hundred years but because these older, more intuitive tools allow us to access far greater potentials of that vast wellspring we call human consciousness.

It is perhaps ironic that the advanced human consciousness work of neurophysiologists such as Karl Pribram and Roger Sperry, who explored the separate functions of the left and right hemispheres of the brain—the right dedicated to the intuitive, the left to the logical—would help to launch a renewed interest in ancient ways of using our minds to deepen our knowledge of the universe. In this respect, tools such as the fetishes tap the resources of the right brain in much the same way that mathematics taps the resources of the left brain.

In the past twenty years or more, my Zuni fetishes have served a function very similar to that of the Celtic runes, the Chinese I Ching, or the Egyptian-inspired Tarot cards. In difficult times, I can turn to fetishes as "mascots" or "talismans" that will comfort or guide me. They provide a pathway to what C. G. Jung called the "collective unconscious" or what the ancients called the "sympathy of all things." And they offer us all access to knowledge far beyond what we have studied in books or experienced firsthand.

I firmly believe that our sincere, open-minded study of the past, aimed at more fully integrating the intuitive aspects of our lives with our practical, everyday experience, is an important step forward in our spiritual evolution. We are in the process of discovering and mastering the full potentials of human consciousness, balancing the functions of the right and left brain, and learning how the individual consciousness is linked with the larger universal consciousness. In the process, we naturally open to the spiritual nature of the universe and of ourselves. We are discovering that we are each expressions of a force much larger than ourselves; in other words, we are discovering our identity with, as the Zunis might put it, the one great system of all-conscious and interrelated life.

In recent years, at major universities and research centers all over the world, human consciousness researchers have shown that our minds are much more than simply the set of mechanistic functions they were once believed to be. Thus, we now know that if we are to use the full potential of human consciousness, we must not limit ourselves to such mental disciplines as math, language, and reasoning. These capacities have been developed over the centuries for making better use of the left-brain potentials of our minds—that is, our linear and logical thought processes. But it is time to once again revivify our intuitive capacities. What skills have we developed for tapping these resources?

It is true that the left-brain disciplines have allowed us to advance tremendously in science, medicine, technology, and commerce. But these processes only scratch the surface of the mind's full capabilities. By exploring meditation, dreams and visions, creative visualization, intuitive insight, the collective unconscious, and divining systems—all ordinarily associated with ancient, primitive cultures—we are learning to use mental tools that will allow our right-brain potentials to be more accessible.

A REALITY SELDOM SEEN BY MODERN SCIENCE

Throughout the Zuni religion, there is great reverence for the unseen world—that is, for those mysterious forces that were created by *A'wonawil'ona* (the Originator of all) and that continue to have an impact on all life. The Zunis' religious beliefs encourage a constant awareness of how dependent we humans are on the natural order and on forces that are mysterious to us. It is interesting to read accounts of former missionaries, traders, and anthropologists who observed Native American practices. These Europeans had great faith in their own ability to conquer and control nature, and their attitude toward the native people's emphasis on living in harmony with the natural order was one of condescension, if not downright disdain and hatred. Today, with the massive environmental problems we are facing, the views of life that have been held by native peoples begin to look a lot more like wisdom than superstition. Indeed, modern science itself has begun to rediscover those revelations instinctively experienced by ancient peoples centuries ago. Albert Einstein paid homage to just such insights when he stated that a "human being is a part of the whole, called by us 'Universe,'" and our feelings of separation from that whole are "a kind of optical delusion of consciousness."[2]

Since the beginning of time, humans have revered the mysterious, acknowledging—though never quite fully grasping—the enigmas of life and death and the creation of the universe itself. Whether through science, the arts, religion, or in our own solitude, we have been attracted to the unexplainable. How did the world begin? What is the force within us that we call life? What is the nature of that intelligence, which must be far greater than our own, that guides the movements of the planets, the seasons, and our own lives? Are there ways in which we, through our own consciousness, are linked with the eternal forces of the universe?

Along with the allure of the mysterious, we long to connect in a special way with what at times seems unknowable. In quiet moments, we may experience—all too briefly!—a fading of the physical boundaries by which we define our everyday lives and a sense that we are in touch with the mysteries. We still may not be able to explain them, but these experiences convince us once again that there is an unseen world that is as real as the ground under our feet.

The Zuni religion suggests that we can remember the time before birth when we were fully at one with the spirit, or consciousness, that exists in all things. This memory, the Zunis hold, is the basis for our infatuation with life's unseen realities. Thus, our attraction to the mysterious may finally prove to be no less than our longing to be joined once again with our source.

THE PURPOSE OF THIS BOOK

I was encouraged to write this book by a friend who has shared my enthusiasm for a variety of ancient oracle systems, including the Zuni fetishes. Both of us have found in such systems a way of accessing the rich creative and spiritual resources that exist within every human being. And we have both noted that effective tools for accessing these resources are difficult to find in contemporary life.

Thus, it is my sincere hope that the information I have tried to pass along in these pages will help to fill this gap, for I believe that by striving for a deeper understanding of ourselves, as well as of the universe in which we live, we can ultimately make each moment of our lives on this planet more fulfilling, more pleasurable, and easier.

My own exploration of Native American religions, and of shamanism in particular, has been a part of my search for guidance toward enjoying a more loving relationship with nature, with this beautiful blue planet that is our Mother. I have found in many of the shamanic practices the promise of a new way of looking at the world, one that can teach us alternatives to the often exploitative practices of our Western European heritage.

While the Zunis emphasize our dependence on mysterious spiritual forces outside us, they also believe that we have the power to bring ourselves into a harmonious and nurturing relationship with the deities associated with those forces. By establishing a friendly relationship with these deities, we can ultimately find comfort, happiness, and peace.

To understand the Zuni fetish, we need to see it in its original context, assisting humanity in honoring the mysteries of nature. These small, often crude carvings can assist us in healing our relationships with ourselves, each other, our planet, and the source of all life itself. The fetishes can help us make more informed decisions about the future, get more in touch with our life purpose, and through them we can receive guidance and support from forces greater than ourselves. They offer us direction in our exploration of the inner world where the paths of our daily lives are charted. Above all, they are gifts that allow us to see the unknown and mysterious in a new light.

Every author has goals that he or she probably has no right to impose on the reader. Still, I find myself hoping that this book will help its readers to establish new and closer relationships with those eternal forces that are responsible for life on this planet. I can only trust that you, with my best intentions in mind, will forgive whatever vanity this hope may conceal.

ONE

THE COUNCIL OF HUMANS, FETISHES, AND GODS

To find the center and live in balance, you've got to jump out of your skin.
Look at the world through the clear eyes of the soaring Eagle
and the blind eyes of burrowing Mole.

—AWAHAKEEWAH

IT WAS 4:00 A.M. *The light of the new day was only now reaching the edge of the desert, so the morning was still cool. The old woman, Red Deer, sat under the piñon tree at the side of her tiny house. On the ground in front of her, she had made a little circle of rock figures. There were six figures in all, none much bigger than a baby's fist. Each one was crudely carved. Long ago, maybe as long as a hundred years before, someone had taken rocks whose natural shapes had suggested the bodies or heads of animals. The fetish maker had then used a blade of flint to scrape notches in the stone to suggest a leg or a mouth or the crook of a neck. Time had polished the rock figures so that now they were smooth and shiny, the way they might be if the waters of a swift mountain stream had washed over them for many years.*

Two of the rock figures, Mountain Lion and Wolf, had eagle feathers and beads of turquoise and coral tied to their backs with rawhide that was brittle with age. These two had belonged to Red Deer's grandfather and perhaps to her great-grandfather before that, and Red Deer could not look upon them without thinking of her many ancestors and how she stood in a wide stream of ancient wisdom that flowed through the middle of all life.

Red Deer sat facing north. Now she looked down and spoke the names of each fetish as if to get its attention. "Yellow Lion, listen to me," she said. Then, "Listen, Black Bear! Listen, Badger! Listen, White Wolf! Listen, Crowned Eagle! Listen, Earth Digger!"

The old woman addressed each of her six rock figures in turn, greeting them as one might greet a respected teacher. Then she took the one she called Black Bear into her hand, pressed it close to her lips, breathed on it for a moment, and then sucked, drawing spiritual sustenance from it. She set Black Bear back in the circle and reached into a small bowl that she had brought with her from the kitchen. She withdrew a handful of corn kernels. She placed two or three kernels in front of each animal as an offering, then looked up at the sky. She closed her eyes and sang. The words to her song were simple: "We walk with the ancients. Yes, yes, most certainly the ancients listen."

She hummed to herself, eyes closed, smiling. As she did, she felt the presence of Marie, her eldest daughter, whom she called White Running Wolf because as a child she had run so beautifully and so fast. In races with the other children at school, she had always won. She ran faster than the boys in her class, which had made many of the boys angry but which had made Red Deer very proud.

White Running Wolf lived a long way away now, in New York City, where Red Deer had never been and was afraid to go. White Running Wolf, who was called by her white name, Marie Sanchez, was a nurse in the surgery department of a large hospital in the middle of the city. Last night Red Deer had a troubling dream about her daughter. She had dreamed that White Running Wolf was grieving the loss of a friend whom she had loved deeply. Her daughter's grief tore at Red Deer's own heart, and she wanted to bring peace and healing to both of them.

Red Deer spoke with the fetish she called Crowned Eagle, who told her he would fly to White Running Wolf's home and comfort her in her *grief. He would remind her that her grief would pass, and she would soon be free to return to her work of helping people at the hospital.*

Red Deer then spoke with Yellow Lion. He told Red Deer that she had taught her daughter well and that White Running Wolf did not need her to be her guardian anymore. Although Red Deer's prayers would help, her daughter was strong and would know the medicine for healing the pain she felt in her heart.

Black Bear offered Red Deer comfort for her own heart, reminding her that when winter came it marked a time to be silent within, to wait for the new life that would come after Mother Earth's long sleep. The darkness and cold in her daughter's heart would soon pass, and by spring her mourning period would be over. Red Deer should not be concerned but should remember that her own strength would go to White Running Wolf, carried by Crowned Eagle, if she simply trusted in her daughter to heal the wound of the great loss she had suffered.

When she had finished talking with her fetishes, Red Deer wrapped them in a buckskin cloth worn smooth by the years and tied up the bundle with a leather thong. Then she put her bundle in a clay pot, the fetish jar that had been shaped by her great-grandmother's hands long ago, and placed it carefully under her bed.

When Red Deer's children were growing up and living at home with her, they had made fun of her when she spoke to "her rocks," as they called the fetishes. But talking with them always brought Red Deer comfort and gave her strength. She let her children tease her, but she also told them that speaking with the fetishes helped her to remember the wisdom of the ancients. It was important for them to remember this wisdom, too. The fetishes did not let her forget the teachings that had offered comfort and strength to every generation since the beginning of time. Besides, the fetishes had never lied to her, and even her children admitted that their mother learned things through the rocks that she could not have known otherwise.

A week passed and a letter came. Red Deer immediately took the letter into her house and tore it open, knowing it was from White Running Wolf. White Running Wolf told of a terrible accident that had happened in another country. An airplane had crashed and the young woman named Carol, who had been White Running Wolf's friend and roommate in college, had been on it. She had died instantly.

White Running Wolf's grief had been almost more than she could bear. Carol had been her closest friend for many years, and Marie had come to depend on her to talk things over when she was troubled. White Running Wolf said that when she first heard of her friend's death, now more than a week ago, she had felt exhausted and weak and had been unable to go to work. She had stayed at home and wept. Then she had awakened early one morning feeling she was no longer alone. Her healing had begun almost immediately, and now she was back at work, feeling sad but strong.

The letter closed with a thank-you. Marie said, "I am pretty sure you sensed my troubles and spoke with your rock animals. Thank them for me, and thank you for the healing you have sent me."

Red Deer smiled, then went outside to sit under the piñon tree and give thanks to the rocks in her own way.

THE FETISH AS HELPER

For the people of Zuni (called the *Ashiwi,* meaning "Flesh of the Flesh,") the fetish is a way of accessing ancient wisdom and aligning oneself with natural forces. These little stone carvings are revered as tools for exploring one's inner world or for asking spiritual helpers from the "unseen world" for their assistance in everyday life. The carvings, resembling animals that appear in the Zunis' physical environment as well as in their mythology, act as mediators between the human world and the world of intuitive knowledge that nurtures the creative spirit in all of us.

For the modern Zuni who adheres to the traditional spiritual beliefs, the fetish is not considered to have power until it has been sanctified by the appropriate person within the community. Until then, the figure itself is little more than a carving of an animal. For this reason, many modern artisans will claim only that they carve animal figures and that it is not their place to "make fetishes." Similarly, they will decorate their carvings with bits of turquoise, coral, shell, or even "points" or arrowheads, but rarely with feathers since these are to be added only in the ceremonies that give a fetish its power.

At its most rudimentary level, the Zunis' consultation with a fetish might be likened to the act of prayer, meditation, or contemplation; it is essentially the same process by which religious peoples of both the East and the West acknowledge their reverence for their spiritual principles or their saints. Anthropologist Tom Bahti states that the fetish was intended to "assist man, that most vulnerable of all living creatures, in meeting the problems that face him during his life."[1]

The earliest fetishes were found objects, rather than the crafted figures that they are today. They were natural stones in the shapes of animals and were believed to be actual petrifications of animals that had once lived. As such, they contained the *potential* or spirit of the animal they physically resembled. The fetishes put one in touch with the characteristic qualities and the innate wisdom of the figures they depicted. The qualities and wisdom associated with each animal were derived from the Zunis' astute observation of the natural world, as well as from their mythology.

The abstract or symbolic form of the wolf fetish, for example, connected its owner with wolf in any of its other forms—from the flesh and blood wolf, to the hunter's thought of wolf, to the earliest spiritual (*ahai*) manifestations of wolf. In this way, the hunter who consulted with the Wolf fetish could gain great power over his prey.

In one of the legends that Frank Hamilton Cushing reported in his book *Zuni Breadstuff,*[2] a coyote meets with a young man who is described as a real bungler as a hunter. In this humorous but highly instructive tale, the young man is hunting for a deer to kill and bring back to his tribe, but he is doing a very poor job of it. Coyote, who is well known and respected as a deer hunter, instructs the young man, helping him to track the deer, kill it, perform the necessary rituals of thanks to the deer for its sacrifice, and then pay homage to the gods by casting cornmeal about at the site of the kill. After all this, Coyote further instructs the young man:

Now pray thy father (thy child, the slain deer), that in his walks abroad he shall remember thy name—which tell him; shall commend thee to the creatures of game, in order that thou shalt unfailingly enjoy their favor. Plant with prayer and yearning the plumed sticks of investiture and scatter abroad thy favor of prayer meal. Thou receivest flesh wherewith to add unto thy own flesh. For this thou shalt always confer in return that which giveth new life to the hearts of slain creatures. Hereafter thou shalt hunt alone, carry with thee the fetish of a Prey-god, one of them cannot always be with you as I am today. Thus by our forms, made stony in the days of creation, shalt thou be minded to invest us with treasure, offer us favor, and plant for us prayer sticks and heart-plumes. See! Thou will then possess the goodwill of both the Prey-beings and their prey, and trebly gifted as a hunter wilt thou be.

In considering the Zunis it is important to remember that this is a people who live very close to the earth. If you study their mythology you will discover their great affinity with animals and plants, with the earth itself, and the forces of nature, such as lightning, the wind, the rain, and the sun, and even with the rocks under their feet. If you have this affinity, the act of holding in your hand the fetish of an eagle, for instance, will allow you to be touched by the spirit of that bird, with its ability to soar high on the winds and to look down and observe the tiniest movements below it; it will help you to experience how it might feel to live in balance and harmony between the sky and the earth. To possess an Eagle fetish is to share Eagle's power, to be able to call upon its spirit and knowledge to provide understanding, to assist in healing, or to rally luck for a hunt. To fully appreciate the power of the eagle was to heighten one's awareness of the seemingly infinite manifestations of Awonawilona, the Creator.

The power of different fetishes varies tremendously. Usually, the most powerful are those that are the most abstract, amorphous, natural, and thus the most mysterious. However, each fetish's power depends primarily on its ability to evoke for its owner the spirit of the animal or natural force the figure represents, thus allowing the owner to feel connected with *ahai*, the spiritual web created by Awonawilona, which moves through all things.

Early missionaries in the Southwest mistakenly believed that the fetishes were "graven images" and that the Native Americans worshipped these little figures as idols. But this was not the case. The idol-worshiper looks upon the object itself as a god or deity, while the fetishist looks upon the object as a representation of a spirit or force. It is through their fetishes that the Ashiwi honor the power of the spirit or whatever natural force the fetish represents and evokes. But these spirits do not have the power of a deity. Except under special circumstances, their power is little more than what the animal would possess in real life, or in mythology.

While not graven images, the original fetishes did play an important role in the shaping of the Zuni peoples' religion and in supporting the social mores that evolved from it. According to the Ashiwi way, outlined by a complex cosmology and religion, one's work with the fetishes must always be healing and positive. All human ills are perceived as the result of failing to observe nature's laws and thus of being out of balance with the natural forces; this imbalance is the product either of ignorance or of some selfish quality such as greed, jealousy, or dishonesty. One's work with the fetish is aimed at maintaining or restoring, if it has been violated or lost, one's balance with nature.

The fetish reminds us that we are not alone and that life on this planet did not begin with us. It reminds us that many generations of innumerable species have preceded us and many are to follow, and each of our lives is but a minuscule portion of a system so vast and mysterious that only the most arrogant among us would claim to understand it or dare to control it for selfish gain. The Zuni religion and cosmology do not seek to harness the mysteries or control them; they strive instead to acknowledge, honor, and preserve them.

THE FETISH AS CONDUIT TO ANOTHER REALITY

At the very least, the fetish provides its owner with a reference point for navigating in the "unseen reality"—that is, the creative or spiritual world, or the world of dream—where there are no objective boundaries. The Zunis believe that everything in the universe, from natural forces such as lightning, wind, and great droughts, on the one hand, to rocks, animals, rivers, and human beings, on the other, is a highly individualized, concrete expression of nonhuman forces that exist in this unseen reality.

For the contemporary mind, the concept of an unseen reality is not easy to grasp. However, we encounter the unseen reality in virtually everything we do, just as people did in primitive times. For example, we encounter this unseen reality the moment we stop and ask the source of the objects around us. We quickly realize that all things produced by humans, whether they are works of art, great buildings, automobiles, bridges, roads, or even children, could not have come into being had they not been preceded by thoughts and feelings—and these are all expressions of the unseen reality. All that humankind makes grows from thought.

For the Ashiwi, the unseen reality, with all its various forces and spirit forms, originated in and is constantly a part of a larger force, which is comparable to the Tao of ancient Chinese thought but for which the Ashiwi have no name. The Zuni religion teaches that we all live in an infinite sea of spirit; within this sea there appear endless physical and energetic forms, from the tiniest of entities, comparable to subatomic particles, to the countless animal and vegetable species, to the vast heavens themselves, which are filled with forms and phenomena that we can only begin to imagine.

Ashiwi theology describes the various life forms and how they came into being, but it has no word that exactly parallels the Judeo-Christian concept of God. Instead, their cosmology begins with an ambiguous description of a formless mist and the presence of Awonawilona, who is the "container of all things." Everything created in the universe emanates from Awonawilona, including the life spirit that animates all, linking humanity with all of nature and the cosmos. The Zuni word for this universal spirit is *ahai*, roughly translated as the "life force in all beings." As Frank Cushing stated in a report to the secretary of the Smithsonian Institution in 1880, *ahai* is the spirit of the "one great system of all-conscious and interrelated life."[3]

This aspect of the Zuni cosmology roughly parallels the concept of *logos* (the Word) as expressed in the Gospel of John in the Christian Bible: "When all things began, the Word (Logos) already was. The Word dwelt with God, and what God was, the Word was. The Word, then, was with God at the beginning, and through him all things came to be; no single thing was created without him. All that came to be was alive with his life, and that life was the light of men. The light shines on in the dark, and the darkness has never mastered it" (John I:1–5).

MYSTERIES OF LIFE AND FORM

Both Zuni and Christian cosmologies struggle to express the essential mystery of the universe—that is, how form of any kind could have emerged from formlessness. In striving to answer this question, we humans attempt to transcend the limits of the human mind so that we might begin to grasp the concept of formlessness itself. This struggle is, I believe, at the core of every spiritual belief system, ancient or modern, in the world. This mystery lies beneath every question humanity has ever asked about the nature of the universe.

Throughout the Zuni tales and legends, there is a clear recognition of this mystery. Their stories reflect a deep respect for and understanding of the ways in which form is constantly changing—from thought or spirit to physical form, from physical form to death, from decay to rebirth, from a dry, seemingly inert seed to a lively and fertile plant that bears corn, which in turn provides nutrients that nurture the life spirit in humans, and so on.

Certain beings in the Zuni mythology have the capacity to play with form and formlessness, to manipulate them according to their will. These beings are known as "surpassing beings," and are *hlimna*, a word the non-Zuni finds all but impossible to pronounce. In his "Outlines of Zuni Creation Myths,"[4] Cushing's translation of one Zuni myth describes two surpassing beings. The legend proclaims that they were "*hlimna* (changeable), even as smoke in the wind; transmutable as thought, manifesting themselves in any form at will, like as dancers may by mask-making."

Like rocks, animals, or any other entity in the universe, human beings are a part of the infinite sea of spirit that the Zunis describe; we are constantly both in it and of it. When we view our lives within the grander scheme, measuring time not in decades but in thousands of years, we see that we, too, are *hlimna*. We have taken many forms in the past and will take many others in the future. This concept reminds me of one of my favorite Ralph Waldo Emerson quotations: "Everything in Nature contains all the powers of Nature. Everything is made of one hidden stuff."[5]

Just as our knowledge of or our empathy with any form or force can be evoked through our words, so can this knowledge and empathy be evoked through the fetish. By holding the fetish in our hands or placing it before us as we pray or meditate, we can bring ourselves more and more into alignment with the spirit of the animal it represents or with the set of principles that it symbolizes for us. And it is through this alignment with spirit or important principles that we experience the fetish's greatest power. The parallel in our everyday life might be the contemplation of an object such as a work of art, a great building, or even an automobile, if this contemplation leads us to imagine all that occurred between the moment when it was first conceived and the present. Through such an exercise, we begin to appreciate the degree to which we are dependent on the unseen reality to accomplish even the simplest act.

JOURNEY TO THE MIDDLE PLACE

The Zunis live in the town of Zuni in western New Mexico, south of Gallup and west of Albuquerque. Although they are generally classified as one of the Pueblo ("village") peoples, their language is quite different from any of those spoken by other Pueblos of the region. In fact, the Zuni language is so very different from any other Native American language that some anthropologists have speculated that they came from an entirely different ancestral lineage.[6]

Today, as in ancient times, the Zuni people refer to their home country as Halóna Itiwana *It'a-a-na*, the Middle Place. Legend has it that a giant Water Strider, a mythical creature, helped them locate the Middle Place by stretching his many legs to the outermost edges of the earth. He then lowered his body, and the point where he touched the earth became known as Itawana. The legend states that this is to be the Zunis' home until the end of time. The term *Middle Place* comes up throughout the many legends told by the Zunis, and there is much debate about exactly what this term means. Some say it means the "center" of the world, while others say it stands for the "heart" of the world. Given the Zunis' emphasis on achieving and maintaining balance with the natural forces, we can speculate that it was originally intended in the sense of home or center being the place where one found balance, the place of beginnings and endings.

The Zunis' land is a high plateau, a rugged terrain of sandstone mesas, most of which are covered by low brush, juniper, and piñon. At the higher elevations, near the continental divide, there are ponderosa pine forests. In the valleys along the divide there are many small family farms that survive in this arid region only through careful irrigation. It is estimated that the Zuni people first appeared in this region around 1300.

During the sixteenth century, the Spaniards explored the Zuni territory, finding the Native Americans living in what the explorers called the Seven Cities of Cibola. The Spaniards mistakenly took this area to be a legendary "Lost City of Gold" and raided it for its treasures, which did not exist. While their towns were being razed by the newcomers, the Native Americans fled to the top of Thunder Mountain, just as they had for many centuries whenever danger threatened. They eventually came together again in the single village of "The Middle Place," which is now the most populous area in the land of the Zunis. Today the Zunis have the largest population in their history, numbering over 6,000. It is interesting to note that when Frank Hamilton Cushing lived with them he estimated their population at 1,800. Today the Zuni people are self-supporting, obtaining most of their income as wage earners, potters, silversmiths, cattle ranchers, and, of course, fetish makers.

While the production of fetishes for a large market is a relatively new endeavor for the Zunis, they long ago established themselves as master fetish makers in the Native American world, and their fetishes continue to be desired by other tribes. For example, the Navajos seek out Zuni fetishes depicting sheep, goats, cattle, or horses to protect their animals from disease and to encourage their propagation.

HOW FETISHES CAME TO BE

In Zuni mythology, Awonawilona created Father Sun, the Moon, and two superhuman beings, *Shi-wa-ni* and *Shi-wa-no-kia*, who in turn created the earth and the starry skies. Deep within the earth, Shiwani and Shiwanokia also produced the creatures that would one day become human beings, insects, and other animals.

When human beings had evolved into a form resembling their present one, Awonawilona sent a number of deities to Mother Earth for the good of all. At that time, the world consisted mostly of mud and was inhabited by huge beasts that made human life very difficult. In order to make life easier for the humans, Father Sun sent Shiwani and Shiwanokia to assist in the hardening of the entire world, turning the huge beasts into stone. In the process, the spirits of the animals were permanently captured inside; thus, on a spiritual level they continued to be alive, at one with the natural world and able to act as mediators between humans and entities in the unseen world.

There came to earth at that time Poshaiankia, the father of the Medicine Societies. He brought with him the powers to make peace and war and to heal illness of all kinds. He spoke to all the petrified beasts, telling them that from this day forward they should serve humans and no longer be hostile toward them. The animals agreed to do this.

When Poshaiankia came to earth, he appointed certain animals to be his guardians. He instructed each one to take a guard position around him. He told Mountain Lion, "Since you are the Master Hunter, stout of heart and quick of mind, I assign you to be Guardian of the North."[7] To Black Bear he assigned the duty of Guardian of the West, the direction in which the day ends. To White Wolf he assigned the duty of Guardian of the East, from whence the new day comes. And to Badger he assigned Guardianship of the South. Lastly, he made Bald Eagle the guardian of Above and Mole the guardian of Below.[8]

When communicating with an animal fetish, the Zuni considers not only the fetish's obvious animal identity but also its mediating ability between humans and the higher forces of the natural world. Both conscious and unconscious knowledge are associated with each fetish figure. For example, a bear fetish might be chosen as a mediator for a variety of reasons: first, of all animals that are native to Zuni territory, it most closely resembles human beings and for that reason is most open to communion with them; second, because it is more mysterious and spiritually powerful than human beings, it is able to commune with the higher powers, thus creating a link between humans and those powers; and third, the bear has been defined as having certain legendary attributes with which the person consulting it is familiar.

GUARDIANS OF THE SIX DIRECTIONS

In Zuni mythology, there are said to be six directions; North, South, East, West, Above, and Below. Each of these is associated with a color: yellow, red, white, blue, "many-colored," and black, respectively. The directions and their colors figure in stories, rituals, and the design of fetishes for specific purposes. For example, in some legends, Mountain Lions of different colors guard the six directions:

yellow Mountain Lion to the North, blue Mountain Lion to the West, white Mountain Lion to the East, and red Mountain Lion to the South. The spotted or many-colored Mountain Lion is the guardian of the Upper Regions while black Mountain Lion is the Guardian of the Lower Regions. Mountain Lion is chosen as the Guardian figure for very specific virtues, which include stealth, ferociousness, a highly developed territorial sense, and powerful instincts for detecting danger.

Each of the directions has a spiritual significance within the Zuni religion, the most obvious ones being the natural phenomena associated with them. The East, for example, is the direction from which comes the Sun, one of the most powerful and revered natural forces and deities in the Zuni religion; conversely, it is spiritually, then, the Sun that is seen as the *source* of all life, with the East being a place of beginnings, the West being a place of finishes. When the Zuni addresses a fetish that is associated with one of the directions and that thus represents one of these great forces in the natural order, then, of course, that person addresses much more than just an animal. He or she may be asking the fetish to be a mediator between humanity and the great spirit of, let us say, the rising sun of the east, the cold winds of the north, the deities of the sky above, and the most ancient of deities in the earth below.

In addition to evoking the spirit or the assigned spiritual role of the animal that a fetish represents, a person who contemplates that object can also connect him or her with the spirit of the material from which the fetish itself is made, with the spirit of the craftsperson who shaped it, and with the ancestors who owned and used the fetishes before. Thus, a fetish made of clay connects its owner with the earth itself and with legends about the muddy earth that was dried to make life easier for humans; an ancient fetish made and used by great shamans connects its owner with the shamans' powers and with the generations that have passed since they lived.

When people began shaping rocks with their own hands, crafting them from stone, wood, and other materials, it was believed that these fetishes had less power than those found objects whose resemblance to animals had been created by the forces of nature. However, there were then and continue to be now fetish makers whose powers are great because they have special wisdom about the animals, about their own healing capacities, and about the mythical or spiritual forces they represent. A person who owns a fetish crafted by such a person is also able to share in the craftsperson's healing power or special wisdom.

SACRED CONNECTIONS WITH THE FETISH

For the Zuni, the relationship a person establishes with his or her fetishes is important, for it determines whether or not he or she will enjoy success in hunting or healing. While the fetish is believed to guide each individual toward success, if a desired result is not obtained the fetish is not thought to be at fault. Rather, if one meets with failure, he or she should seek the cause within. Perhaps the person asking for help from the fetish was not of "good heart" when he or she asked for assistance, or the ceremony itself was not conducted properly. A Zuni usually found the reason for failure within himself or herself, either through self-examination or by going to a shaman, or priest, who assisted that person in restoring his or her balance with the natural forces.

The Zuni people's stories, rituals, and spiritual practices teach a highly moral way of living, at the center of which is reverence for all of life. The Zunis' rich oral tradition tells of the misfortunes suffered by men and women who forgot or who lost touch with the main principle of their religion: that we are all expressions of Awonawilona and that to be reverent toward Awonawilona, one must be reverent toward the animals, the plants, the sun, the moon, the cosmos—and even toward one's enemies.

Even when, in ancient times, the Zunis made war and took scalps, this reverence for life was expressed through their rituals. Scalps taken by the warriors were brought home and washed in a fetish jar specifically maintained for that purpose. The scalp, like a fetish, was believed to contain the spirit or ghost of the person from whom it was taken. It was handled with great care and respect and was cleansed by the relatives of the warrior who had taken it. The victorious warrior's wife was obligated to go into mourning for a month, just as if she were the dead warrior's own widow. In this way, the Zunis acknowledged the bond they shared even with those enemies that they felt they must destroy.

ALL BEINGS ARE NOT EQUAL

The Zunis believe that while all astral bodies, the sun, the moon, the stars, the sky, Mother Earth, and everything on our planet belong to a single system of interrelated life, there are also degrees of relationship within this system that are based on resemblance. The starting point in this system is humanity, which is the lowest because it is considered the least mysterious and the most dependent. Those animals that most resemble humans are considered closest to humanity in the great web of interrelatedness. Animals, objects, or phenomena that least resemble humans are believed to be the least related and thus more mysterious and more holy. In *Zuni Fetishism*, Ruth F. Kirk states:

> *Thus animals, being mortal, are more nearly related to man than are gods, but the animal is more closely associated with deity than is man because the animal is mysterious and has powers not possessed by man.*[9]

A domesticated animal such as a dog would be viewed as less holy than a snake or other reptile because dogs and humans live together and have a mutual understanding, while reptiles seem alien in the human's world. Since forces in nature such as wind, lightning, and rain are the most mysterious and powerful, they are believed to be closer to the deities than any human or other animal.

There is another level of resemblance that determines the relationships within the web of life. For example, lightning is viewed as being closely related to the snake because they share their characteristic zigzag motion, they strike quickly, and their presence can result in fearful repercussions.

HOW DECORATIONS AFFECT THE POWER OF A FETISH

The power of a fetish might be enhanced by decorating an animal, such as a bear, with objects or designs associated with the most mysterious and therefore most powerful forces. Thus, a fetish, or the fetish jar where it is stored, might be decorated with zigzag patterns evoking the powers of lightning. Similarly, a Zuni might tie a "saddle" of arrowheads onto the backs of an effigy. These objects were not only weapons for self-protection and for killing game, but were also thought to be related to the fangs of the snake. Feathers or claws were something attached in order to evoke the powers of the eagle or other great birds of prey.

ZUNI RESPECT FOR OTHER BELIEF SYSTEMS

For the devout Zuni, the fetish is always holy and potent, always the source of power. To treat any fetish irreverently is viewed in much the same way as a devout Christian might view taking the name of the Lord in vain or desecrating an icon or the altar in a place of worship. One violates taboos regarding the handling of fetishes only at the risk of offending the spirits associated with them. To do so would be considered a selfish and ignorant act, a sign that the perpetrator was "out of balance." And it is the Zuni's balance that keeps him or her in the favor of the natural forces, free of disease and hardship.

It is interesting to note that the Ashiwi show as much reverence for religious objects of non-Zunis as they do for their own. An excellent example of this is found in the story of a *santo* that came into their lives via the Spanish missionaries, following the Pueblo Rebellion of 1680. The *santo*, an image of the Christ child of Our Lady of Atocha, stood approximately a foot tall and was kept surrounded by religious symbols of the Catholic faith. In spite of the fact that the Spaniards had nearly destroyed the Zuni society, the Zunis did not take revenge on ecclesiastical property. The *santo* was ritualistically fed each day, just as any Zuni fetish would be.

In questioning Zuni people about their treatment of the *santo*, Ruth F. Kirk reported that the Native Americans were not certain "how much good or ill might emanate from the white man's fetish but they thought it advisable not to take any chances, so observed the rules that apply to their own holy objects."[10] The person who told this to Kirk added that the *santo* was a "good friend" to the Zunis, and they considered it a powerful fetish. Both the Zunis and some of the Spanish Americans living in the area have attributed many miracles to this little saint figure.

Kirk notes further that while the people of Zuni paid homage to the *santo*, its original Christian meaning had undergone some changes in the process of being incorporated into the Zuni belief system. The Zunis' interpretations no longer complied with Catholic thought. For example, they believed the *santo* to be a female deity. Their legend states that this figure was the child of a daughter of the sun, and each fall they performed a ceremonial dance for the *santo* that was thought to bring fertility to both humankind and nature.

SIX CLASSES OF FETISHES AND POWER OBJECTS

There are six categories of fetishes in the Zuni religion. The first category includes masks, costumes, and other sacred objects used in the Kachina ceremonies. The Kachinas are ancestral deities that live beneath the surface of a lake in a place called Kachina Village. At various times throughout the year, the Zuni people don masks and costumes that represent these deities. The actors perform ancient dances in which they imitate the Kachinas; through the ritual, the spirit of the deity enters the actors and transforms them. Between ceremonies, the masks and other sacred objects belonging to the Kachinas, like all other fetishes, are fed, cared for, and offered daily prayers. Though they may be held, attended to, and worn by the individuals who perform the Kachina dances, these objects are considered to be the property of the tribe, not of any one individual.

The second classification of fetish is the *mili*. This is a personal fetish that consists of a perfect ear of corn—one that ends in five symmetrical rows. It may be wrapped with a variety of feathers. It is presented to a young man at the time he is initiated into a religious society. This fetish symbolizes the life-giving power of the supreme being who is the Creator of life. For the person receiving the *mili*, it also symbolizes the corn's spirit or soul. By breathing on it and inhaling with it next to one's lips, a person can gain strength and renew his or her life. The *mili* is destroyed upon the death of its owner, whereupon the seeds of corn that it contains are sown in the fields and the feathers that were once attached may be used in making prayer sticks.

Prayer sticks, consisting of a wooden shaft, like an arrow, decorated with feathers, comprise a third classification of fetishes, though they are more properly classified as amulets. They do not, like fetishes, have spirits residing within them. Rather, they are simply offered to please the spirits, attract their attention, and earn their favor.

A fourth classification of fetishes are the so-called concretion fetishes. These are rocks that resemble organs in the human body and are described as being petrified organs of the gods. They are generally described as belonging to deities that once walked on the earth, and thus they are considered useful in making contact with these deities in their spiritual form.

A fifth group of fetishes are the *ettowe*. An *ettone* (the singular form of *ettowe*) consists of several short reeds wrapped in cotton string to form a round, compact bundle. The *ettowe* are used in rainmaking ceremonies, which are critical in the arid valley of Zuni, New Mexico.

The sixth classification of Zuni fetishes consists of the "priesthood fetishes," and it is these with which we will be most concerned in this book. *Priesthood fetish* is something of a misnomer since these fetishes are not used exclusively for priestly rites. Fetishes in this group include likenesses of animal figures, such as Mountain Lion, Bear, Coyote, Badger, Wolf, and Eagle, like those now being carved by Zuni craftspeople and sold to people in the cities.

The most holy and therefore most powerful of these fetishes are those that have been in the possession of the tribe since the beginning of time. Generally, the newer and more realistic the fetish, the less its power.

The priesthood fetishes come in many different sizes. They range from three to twelve inches in length. Each represents an animal that is believed to have well-defined powers. They usually have faces that resemble humans, animals, or sea serpents. If the actual animals have prominent tails, the fetish may have a tail, too, or the shape of a tail may simply be etched into the main body of the fetish. In the old tradition, the fetish was also given an anus, indicated by a hole under the tail, acknowledging the biological functions of the spirit that lives within. Most old fetishes are girded around their bellies with cotton thread (the modern ones use materials such as monofilament fish line) that holds feathers, fragments of turquoise, beads of various materials such as coral or shell, arrowheads, or other objects.

The body of the fetish may be shaped of bone, shell, clay, stone, or other materials. Many different adornments may be attached to the fetish, some of them to strengthen it, as we have already noted, and some simply as votive offerings, given in appreciation of the fetish's service to its owner. Most shell or turquoise beads found tied to modern fetishes would be classified as votive offerings, while arrowheads, feathers, or bones (everything from vertebrae to bones from the ear of the animal represented by the fetish) are attached to enhance the fetish's powers.

Occasionally the body of the fetish is decorated by etched or painted lines. These may depict the feathers or pinions of a bird, or they may echo traditional decorations used in ceremonial dress, masks, or other sacred objects. One of the most commonly seen decorations of this kind is the "heart-line arrow," a single line that runs from the tip of the fetish's nose or mouth directly back, on each side, to the area of the heart. At the heart is found the pattern of an arrowhead. This heart line suggests the breath or life force—the spirit—of the fetish. Since the heart-line arrow resembles the shape of the snake and of lightning, a fetish decorated in this way is considered very powerful.

Although the power of each fetish varies greatly, even anthropologists and other scientific observers such as Frank Hamilton Cushing, Tom Bahti, and Ruth F. Kirk have reported feeling "a definite, forceful reaction . . . in the presence of these fetishes, especially in handling them."[11]

THE CARE AND FEEDING OF FETISHES

Traditionally, each fetish must be ritualistically fed. Each day it receives meals, often at the same time that the family owning or caring for the fetish eats. These meals consist of food placed on a piece of paper or pottery and presented to the fetish. The food is usually cornmeal, sometimes mixed with crushed turquoise and shells, but the fetishes may also receive whatever the family is eating at that time. One observer with whom I spoke told of having dinner with a Zuni family. On his way home from work, the husband had stopped at a fast-food restaurant for a bucket of fried chicken and french fries. Before sitting down to eat, the husband ritualistically fed tiny portions of this same food to the group of fetishes in the family's possession.

The ritual food is left out for the fetishes for fifteen to thirty minutes, during which time the fetishes receive the spirit of the food and thus are nourished. Afterward, the physical scraps of the food, which are all that remains, are thrown away. Traditionally, these scraps were thrown in the river or buried in the ground, but they could not be burned since it was believed that the spirits of the departed live in the air and would be offended if they were offered food that no longer contained nourishment. Drained of its nourishment, the ritual food is not even considered fit for dogs.

FETISH SETS

Fetishes are used in sets that usually consist of from three to seven figures and a clay fetish jar that houses them. An exception to this is the hunter's medicine bundle, which consists of a leather pouch worn around the neck and containing a number of small fetishes or power objects that would help the hunter as he went out on his quests for food.

Fetish jars measure up to approximately fourteen inches in height and sixteen inches in diameter. For the fetishes' comfort, the bottom of the jar is lined with down, which may be sprinkled with powdered turquoise or shell. In the side of most jars is a hole that is between one and four inches in diameter, through which the fetishes can be fed. Traditionally, the mouth of the jar was carefully covered, usually with a piece of deerskin from an animal that had been ritualistically killed. The fetishes were placed inside the jar facing outward.

Ruth F. Kirk reports examining at least two fetish jars that were tipped on their sides instead of standing upright. These had no feeding hole, but the fetishes inside pointed outward toward the open mouth of the jar. Both of these jars contained natal fetish sets (used in connection with births in the tribe), and the shape of the jars resembled the uterus.

The outside surface of the fetish jar is typically quite plain except that turquoise dust and fragments may be pressed into the clay before firing. Some jars are decorated with feathers or are etched with the symbols for lightning, wind, or other natural forces, and some even have special fetishes that guard the mouth of the jar or the feeding hole.

The jars are washed frequently, usually as part of the ceremony prescribed for the use of the fetishes that reside within them. Each fetish set has a particular purpose, ranging from initiating young people into a clan or religious order, to healing disease, to aiding in pregnancy and birth, to the washing of scalps taken in battle.

DAILY PRAYERS

Traditionally, if an owner hoped to gain the favor of the spirits that lived within his or her fetishes, then he or she would take great care to feed them, keep them safely and comfortably housed, and pay homage to them through prayers to the natural spirits or forces they represented. When working with the fetishes to gain power before a hunt, for example, one would begin with a song, chant, or prayer that acknowledged the spirit of the fetish as well as the natural forces that were responsible for the creation of the animal represented. In his report to the Bureau of American Ethnology in 1883, Cushing provided the following "free translation," as he called it, of a song offered at the beginning of a hunt:

> *Why (of course)—*
> *This day, my father (or, my mother), here I, (as if) unexpectedly, meet thee with whatsoever I have made ready of the sacred things of my fathers, the priest gods of the sacred dances, the priest gods of the Prey (beings). These sacred things bringing I have here overtaken thee,*

and with their good fortune I here address thee. Wishing for that
whereby thou has being, I shall go forth from here prayerfully upon the
trails of my earth-mother.

Throughout the whole of this great country, they whereby thou has
being, the deer, by the command of the wind of life (breath), wander
about. It is wishing for their flesh and blood that I shall go forth yon-
der prayerfully out over the trails.

Let it be without fail that thou shall make me happy with that
whereby thou hast being. Grant unto me the light of thy favor.[12]

Following this prayer, the hunter scattered prayer meal in the direction that he planned to begin his hunt. He then chose a particular
fetish, lifted it toward his lips, and breathed in, ritualistically taking
in its spirit. After completing this portion of the ceremony, he pro-
claimed:

Ah! Thanks, my father (or, my mother), this day I shall follow (thee)
forth over the trails. Prayerfully over the trails I shall go out.[13]

After asking for the fetish's guidance, one listened for a sign, which
might come in the form of a "hunch" or other "inner feeling," such
as an inner voice or perhaps a mental picture of how the hunter
might conduct the hunt on the following day. There might also be
prayers for the animal being hunted, which would include a request
to Awonawilona to preserve the soul of the animal that the hunter
would kill. The hunter frequently ended the ritual by holding the
fetish next to his lips and breathing, again inhaling the power of its
spirit.

Cushing's 1883 report describes in great detail how the Zunis used
animal fetishes to help them during their hunts. When a hunter decided to go out to pursue an animal, he would choose to work with a
fetish that represented the animal that ordinarily hunted that species.
If the hunter wanted to hunt rabbits on a particular day, he might
choose any one of the fetishes representing animals that hunted the
rabbit, but he might also consult ancient legends to seek guidance in

his choice of fetishes. If the hunter was after jackrabbits, for example, he might ask for Eagle's assistance, since according to most Zuni legends Eagle was the master jackrabbit hunter. If the hunter was after antelope, he would probably ask for Wolf's assistance, since that animal was acknowledged by the Zunis as the master antelope hunter.

Most hunters had a variety of fetishes in their possession, although any individual might have his own favorites, chosen for any number of reasons, ranging from what legend dictated to how well the hunter felt he communicated with a particular fetish. Before the hunt, the hunter ritualistically fed his fetishes, placed them in a circle where he might chant to them, and then "breathed its breath," pressing the nose of the fetish to his own mouth and inhaling the fetish's spirit. The same would be done with the real animal when the hunter made his kill; at that time the hunter would offer thanks not only to the fetishes and the deities but also to the spirit of the dead animal.

There might be several types of hunting fetishes in the leather pouch that the hunter wore around his neck. There were fetishes that represented both the hunter and the hunted. When the hunt was successful, the prey fetish, as a reward, would be dipped in the blood of the killed animal; prayers were also offered to this fetish so that the animal's soul might pass forth, to be preserved and immortalized by receiving a new body in the near future.

While the fetishes used for the hunt were always chosen for their prowess with the particular animal being hunted, they also had qualities of their own that might be applied to initiation rites, healing, fertility, control of the weather, or childbirth. Thus, just as real animals or people have individualized traits and personal histories, so, too, did the fetishes.

The strength, intelligence, and agility of Mountain Lion, for example, might be called upon when one was faced with difficult negotiations with a relative with whom one had a serious dispute. One might call upon Eagle, on the other hand, to fly off on a great journey where he or she might accomplish a special errand, as in the story at the beginning of this chapter. Each fetish animal had these more abstract or legendary qualities and meanings that made the fetish relevant in a wide variety of applications.

ANNUAL CEREMONY OF THE FETISHES

Each year, usually around the winter solstice, the people of Zuni observe what they call *We-ma-a-wa u-pu-k'ia,* or the Day of the Council of the Fetishes. On this day, all the fetishes belonging communally to the tribe or privately to individual tribal members are brought to a symbolic altar on the floor of the council chamber. Animals are arranged according to their type and color on slats placed on the floor. Bird fetishes are suspended in the air, usually by cotton strings.

The ceremonies last through most of the night, with each member of the tribe approaching the altar, addressing the assembly of fetishes with long prayers, then scattering prayer meal over them. Songs and chants are sung, with participants imitating as closely as possible the movements and cries of the animals represented.

"The Day of the Council of the Fetishes" ends with a great feast. Tiny portions of the food from the feast are fed to the fetishes, after which the scraps are disposed of in accordance with the rules of the tribe.

In all rituals surrounding the fetishes, the ceremonies, songs, dances, and offerings are ultimately addressed to Awonawilona, whose spirit or life force permeates the land, the sky, the fetishes, the animals they represent, all the natural forces, and humanity itself, linking all of us as one. Here, as elsewhere, the Zuni ceremonies remind the faithful of the importance of balance in all things, including the use of fetishes. The ceremonies remind everyone that we are all expressions of Awonawilona; it would be arrogant to assume otherwise. There are many instructive stories in the Zuni culture that tell of men and women who acted vainly, attempting to assume powers as if they were separate from, superior to, or in competition with Awonawilona. In these stories, the transgressors are always punished in some way, their punishments ranging from lack of luck in the hunt to great droughts that cause the death of plants, animals, and people.

MESSENGERS FROM THE PAST

Many of the ancient ways of the Ashiwi have been lost, though most Zunis continue to honor their traditions and to think of Itiwana, the Middle Place, as their home. Each year the traditional Kachina dances are held, and a surprising number of the rituals and beliefs surrounding the choice of dancers, the initiation of younger people into the dances, and the care of the masks and other sacred objects continue to be respected.

The use of fetishes endures among individuals, but largely they are now used as talismans—that is, as good-luck objects or charms. When Zuni men and women go hunting, they may wear around their necks a leather pouch containing one or more prey fetishes, but the rituals surrounding these fetishes are now remembered by only a few.

On the other hand, Native Americans, as well as whites, still seek out the Zuni fetishes and other Zuni art objects not only for their beauty but also for their ability to remind us of certain natural principles. In our search for life-affirming values during a time when the health of the planet that supports us is at stake, we particularly need the teachings of wise people whose spiritual and ethical beliefs provide a vision of oneness with nature. Perhaps through these ancient teachings we can begin to heal the wounds we have inflicted through our own lack of balance.

THE USE OF THE FETISH IN MODERN LIFE

For most of us, the world of the Ashiwi seems a far cry from our own, and incorporating the principles of this ancient culture into modern life can seem difficult. Yet many of the truths and principles that the Ashiwi practices upheld can be as useful to us as they were to the Zunis hundreds of years ago. Here are just a few examples of how people are using fetishes today:

Brady, the publisher of a sophisticated life-style magazine, keeps his collection of Zuni fetishes on his desk at all times, turning to them throughout the day to remind him to keep things in perspective when the pressure is on. Coyote reminds him to keep his sense of humor and to recognize that even the greatest stress is created in his own mind. His Bear fetish reminds him to be compassionate, even toward his most powerful rivals, recognizing that the alternative—fear, anger, or hatred—only drains everyone's creative energy. His third fetish, Badger, reminds him that he can be assertive without being hostile, uncaring, or destructive.

Alicia, the manager of an engineering staff for a large electronics firm, keeps two fetishes on her desk: the first is a silver hummingbird, not of Zuni origin. The hummingbird is her "power animal"; it helps her find and maintain her own voice and personal identity in a male-dominated world. Her second fetish is a Mountain Lion, chosen because it helps keep her in touch with her ability to set limits with other people and with herself. Early in her career, she often became burned out by taking on other people's work instead of delegating responsibility. She had to develop various skills that allowed her to set boundaries, and Mountain Lion reminds her of these skills.

Barbara, an economist and financial consultant, keeps on her bookshelf a large, original art piece by a contemporary Zuni artist. The figure is that of a buffalo, reminding her of the fate of that animal when it was exploited by eastern hunters in this country. For her, money is like the buffalo, a resource to be valued for what it can contribute to health, happiness, and well-being, rather than something to be ruthlessly exploited. She often tells her clients that she is neither a bull nor a bear when it comes to investing; she is, instead, a buffalo.

In my classes on the use of fetishes, there are often people who are seeking self-knowledge or who are students of various spiritual disciplines. Most of them find it easy to integrate Zuni principles into their own processes. The values, states of mind, and relationships that the Zunis describe are generally in alignment with most personal development practices. This will become increasingly apparent as you read the next chapter and the descriptions of the fetishes in Chapter Four.

As we study Native American spirituality, particularly that of the Zunis, we realize that their goals were highly pragmatic. The Ashiwi lived in a difficult and often inhospitable region of the world, and their daily lives offered little in the way of creature comforts, to say the least. They had to be responsive to the natural world and to be flexible so that they could adapt to extreme seasonal conditions. Yet in spite of difficult conditions, the Zunis' way of life was fulfilling for most; they were, and still are, a spiritual and creative people, whose unpretentious wisdom is reflected in their gentleness, in their reverence for the earth and the forces of nature, and in their humor.

All these are values that can help us address environmental issues so important today and can show us a more loving and caring way to relate to each other.

TWO

HOW TO CONSULT THE FETISHES

My people are a multitude of one.
Many voices are within them.
Many lives they have lived as various Beings.
They could have been a bear, a lion, an eagle or even
A rock, a river or a tree.
Who knows?
All of these Beings are within them.
They can use them any time they want.

—NANCY WOOD[1]

O**N THE PREVIOUS NIGHT,** *Wema Ashiwani had prepared well for the hunt. He had armed himself not only with the necessary weapons but also with his favorite prey fetish, Mountain Lion, to whom he had offered all the appropriate prayers. He had given the sacrifice of a small amount of cornmeal, as prescribed by the elders. And he had stated that his purpose was to pursue a large buck whose tracks he had seen at the edge of his village the day before.*

Before setting out on the hunt, he faced the North, the region that was Mountain Lion's duty to protect, and placed that fetish directly in front of him. Then he placed the fetishes of White Wolf, Wildcat, and

Coyote[2] in a circle he made in the dirt, being careful to set each fetish in the quadrant assigned to it in ancient times by Poshaiankia, the God of the Medicine societies. To the right of his circle of prey fetishes, he placed his Eagle fetish, and to the left of his circle he placed his Mole fetish; these marking the regions known as Above and Below. He then removed his woven headband, placed it on the ground before him, and uttered the following prayer:

"Today, Father, I come here with my weapons and my prey fetish, and have prepared myself with all the sacred dances and prayers that the priest gods have taught me. I pray to thee that I might have good fortune on my hunt over the trails of my earth mother."

The hunter then scattered prayer meal in the direction in which he had decided to proceed with his hunt and where, on the previous day, he had picked up the trail of the deer. He took Mountain Lion in his hand, pressed it to his lips and sucked, as if receiving its breath. This done, he exclaimed, "Ah, I thank you, my father, that this day you shall guide me in my hunt."

Wema Ashiwani then placed his fetish in a crescent-shaped pouch made of buckskin, which he wore suspended from a leather thong around his neck, placed in such a way that it rested over his heart.

As he set out on his journey, the hunter stopped a little way from his village and picked a few thin leaves from the heart of a yucca plant. As he proceeded along the trail, he studied the ground carefully, following signs such as footprints, droppings, and matted-down grasses where the deer had laid down to rest. The trail turned west two or three miles from the village, then again turned North toward the great forests.

For many hours, Wema Ashiwani traveled in the direction of the Barren Place, until the sun was on his left side. The trail had taken him into the dense forests where many tall trees and thick underbrush shielded the game. Before long, however, Wema Ashiwani caught sight of a matted-down circle of grass where the deer had laid down to rest. The track was fresh here, the droppings still moist, and the grasses bent by the weight of the buck's body were only now beginning to rise. The deer could not be more than a short trek from this place.

Wema Ashiwani took four long strands from the leaves of the yucca plant, tied them together so that they formed a shape like a spider, and placed this object over the spot where he calculated the buck's heart had rested. This spidery figure formed a kind of cage over the imagined heart of the prey. Then the hunter found a forked twig of cedar and stuck it in the ground at an angle so that the forked prong pointed in the direction the animal had gone.

Wema Ashiwani knelt down and made a roaring sound, mimicking the cry of the buck. Then he carefully deposited a sacrifice to the animal, consisting of corn pollen, sacred black war paint, cornmeal made from seed corn, fragments of shell and finely ground turquoise, and beads made of shell or coral. This done, he took out his fetish, breathed on it, and exclaimed, "Everything is ready. The time has come. Now, my father, I and my family hungering for the flesh of thy game animal, I go forth, asking for your blessings and good fortune. I pray for the help of the woods around me that they might reach out with their branches and thick brush and slow down the game I seek."

Wema Ashiwani again pressed his fetish to his lips and breathed in deeply, receiving its breath. He made a low cry four times, a sacred number, in the direction of the buck, again mimicking its cries.

Replacing the fetish in its pouch around his neck, the hunter rose and continued tracking the buck. Another hour passed before he sighted it. It stood in a small clearing, grazing in a narrow meadow of tender grasses. Wema Ashiwani placed an arrow against the string of his bow and crept forward until he was only a short distance from the buck. The deer looked up and saw the hunter standing before him, the string of his bow drawn and ready. In that instant Wema Ashiwani let the arrow fly. The well-aimed shaft pierced the chest of the deer for a clean kill, and the animal fell to its knees almost instantly. Before the breath of life was gone from it, the hunter ran forward, grasped the deer's front feet, placed them behind the animal's head, and pressed its nose to his own lips. He breathed his own wind into the buck's lungs, then inhaled from its lungs as it died. When the spirit had gone from its body, Wema Ashiwani lowered the animal gently to the ground.

This done, he exclaimed, "Ah, thanks, my father, my mother, who grant us our daily bread and the gift of water. Pray that I shall always have the light of your favor as I have had today."

Once the animal was dead, the hunter opened its belly with his knife, pierced the diaphragm, and made an incision in the heart. He then took out his prey fetish, breathed on it, and said, "Now, you shall drink and with the blood of this animal expand your own heart."

Wema Ashiwani pressed Mountain Lion into the heart incision and allowed the fetish to drink the first blood of the kill, just as a real mountain lion would have done. When this reward to the fetish for its assistance was completed, the hunter made an offering to the spirit of the dead buck. This consisted of blood from the deer's own heart, a piece of its ear, some corn pollen, turquoise beads, black paint, and other items like those he had given just before embarking on the hunt. He pressed all these together, making a ball of them, which he buried on the spot where the animal had fallen. Wema Ashiwani then spoke aloud, recounting the adventures of the hunt and giving the following prayer to the spirit of his prey:

"To you, Deer, I wish good fortune and make a sacrifice to you of this sacred corn pollen and other things. With this prayer and these offerings, I pray you good fortune in becoming a new being. May you hear my prayers as you go forth and grant me and my family a good journey over the trail of life."

He then placed his fetish back in its pouch, dressed the deer, and carried it home. He deposited the animal just inside his door. The women came and breathed from the nostrils of the deer as Wema Ashiwani had done. Then they placed the animal so that its head pointed toward the East, laying an ear of corn on either side of its body to signify renewed life. They said short prayers similar to those offered by the hunter, before they prepared the deer to be eaten.

All this having been completed, the hunter returned his prey fetish to the place where it was usually kept when not in use. For Wema Ashiwani, this was a large clay jar decorated with turquoise fragments. In it he also kept the other five prey fetishes, which he fed daily.

As you read the instructions presented in this section of the book, you will find that I have blended ancient Zuni practices with those of modern self-help systems. This combination seems necessary to me partly because the original Zuni symbolism addressed a very different set of issues than those with which most of us are concerned today. But I do not want to imply that the principles and values of the Zunis are a thing of the past. On the contrary, these beliefs and values have much to offer every one of us.

If there is one thing we learn from working with the Zuni fetishes, it is an appreciation for our kinship with every living thing on our planet. If we live according to this perspective, then we do not harm anything. If we take grain from the earth to feed our families, we honor the spirit that makes the growing of the grain possible. We express this reverence not just through prayers and meditation but also through the way in which we care for the land. If we kill an animal to feed our families, we honor the spirit of that animal with a prayer and with a sacrifice of our own, so that its family may continue to thrive. We also protect the homes of these animals, and we are careful not to overhunt them. Even when we must kill a human enemy, we recognize that the life we have taken is sacred; we mourn the death and pray for that warrior's soul, acknowledging the common bond that joins us as one. And we do everything we can to negotiate with our neighbors in order to prevent wars that might result in such killing.

The Zunis who continue to follow the traditional ways make an effort in their daily lives to respect and honor every person, whether he or she is a family member, friend, business associate, or even an enemy. Frank Hamilton Cushing wrote about the Zuni practice of giving an offering of bread to any person who visited one's home. This offering was made as a gesture of respect to the spirit from which we all come and as a sign that our personal differences should never be considered more important than this common spiritual source. Cushing gave examples of how this offering was made and respected even when people had come together because of a serious conflict between them.

To some it may seem farfetched that these same values and practices could serve us today. But they can, and they do. For instance, they can help us heal the environmental disasters that we are presently facing. When we work with the fetishes over a period of time, the insights that emanate from their use begin to reveal a way of thinking, feeling, and relating to the world around us that is healing instead of threatening. Those who recognize and honor our true kinship begin to make very different kinds of choices, opting not to do things that would hurt the earth or the creatures upon it and instead choosing to live in harmony with all. This harmony extends to everything we do, from how we relate to each other to how we relate to great ecosystems such as the deserts or wetlands near our homes or to the distant Amazon rain forests or the great oceans that lie between our continents.

As you become more and more comfortable in your use of the Zuni fetishes, you may first discover subtle changes in your thoughts and feelings and thus begin to relate to yourself in new ways; later, you may discover new ways of relating to those around you; for example, you may be able to make decisions that are less self-centered and more mutually beneficial. Later still, you may find yourself making decisions that honor the planet as a whole. This is all a natural outcome of working with a system of thought that teaches us how to move beyond our five physical senses in order to envision the unseen reality.

In our study of ancient cultures, whether we are looking at that of the Zunis or that of ancient China, India, or Japan, there is always the danger of becoming so enamored of what seems to be a "special" or "unique" set of ideas that we lose sight of the common and essential values that underlie these ideas in every culture. For example, in recent years there has been great interest in the stories of shamanism and sorcery associated with the Native Americans. While our study of these practices has broadened our understanding of realities beyond those with which we are most familiar, we have also sometimes neglected the broader lessons that these traditions have to offer. Taken out of context, the "magic" of sorcery and shamanism becomes little more than an intriguing means of entertainment, and we forget that these transformational processes were initially intended to bridge the chasms we humans have created between the seen and unseen worlds. In the context of the original tradition, they have the power to heal us by reminding us of our spiritual source.

As you begin working with the fetishes, you may find it helpful to keep in mind some of the specific differences between Zuni thought and the modern belief systems with which most of us have grown up. In a million subtle and not so subtle ways, we are taught, from the time we are small children, that we humans can dominate and control the natural world, that we can exploit our natural resources indefinitely, and that it is only a matter of time before all of life's mysteries and uncertainties will be understood by our scientists and harnessed for our own use.

By contrast, in the Native American traditions, one is taught to seek life, to honor the mystery of it without asking why or seeking to dominate and control it. One is taught to observe and appreciate the natural rhythms of life, such as the changing seasons and the cycles of life and death and of illness and health; one learns to value both the great pain of loss and the great joy of love, to honor the powers that make it possible for the life force itself to come into being, and to acknowledge the fact that this same force is present in all that lives, from the lichen growing on a rock in the desert, to a stray cat living in the city, to human beings themselves.

The fetishes best serve us when we are focused on those values and beliefs that respect and honor the mysteries of life. They serve us best when we learn to sit quietly, observing and listening for signs of how we might find greater balance and harmony in our lives.

I suggest that you will find it helpful to read through this section to the end, familiarizing yourself with all the material presented here before you actually start to apply it. In addition, you will find the techniques described here most effective if you become comfortable with at least the six guardian fetishes, described in Chapter Four, before you begin.

THE DIFFERENT CONSULTING SYSTEMS

I describe three different but closely related systems for working with the Zuni fetishes: (1) using them as talismans; (2) using them within the tradition of the Medicine Wheel—which itself will be fully described; and (3) conferencing with them, which is the process of consulting several fetishes jointly.

The instructions for the first system are the simplest, for it consists of using a single fetish of your choosing to bring you courage, good luck, to help you carry a burden, or to strengthen or empower you during challenging times. The second set of instructions uses the Guardians of the Six Regions within the framework of a medicine wheel, a system adapted from ancient Zuni traditions. The third system, conferencing, is a variation on the second. Like the medicine wheel, but in a less structured way, it asks you to use two or more fetishes simultaneously, setting into motion the synergy that occurs in any dialogue among different characters; thus, conferencing with the fetishes resembles the experience of talking over a problem with several experts or friends.

THE SELECTION OF FETISHES

It is not absolutely necessary to have Zuni fetish figures in your possession in order to use these systems, though I recommend that you do start a collection soon if you decide you want to work with them on a regular basis. Genuine Zuni fetishes can be purchased for as little as a couple of dollars, for the tiny bead fetishes used for necklaces and jewelry, up to several hundred dollars for carvings by contemporary Zuni artists. (The Resources section on page 169 lists a few retailers who specialize in fetishes.)

Your fetishes need not be genuine Zuni ones, of course. You can use any objects that "speak" to you, from small china figurines to fetishes you have made yourself from virtually any material. I am reminded here of a story told by Cushing in his report on the medicine bundles of the Zuni shaman. In one bundle, owned by a highly re-spected shaman, Cushing found a small, well-worn rubber mouse. The medicine man considered this humble little figure as powerful as any of the others in his bundle.

If you do not have fetishes and don't wish to purchase or make any, you can simply picture them in your mind. On the inside flaps of the cover of this book, you will find photos of the Guardians of the Directions. You will also find a drawing at the beginning of each reading that will help you visualize the animal you are working with.

After working with the Zuni fetishes for a period of time, you may find it useful to add fetishes of your own, usually objects for which you have a strong emotional attachment or that represent important milestones in your life. For my students, these objects have included everything from a diamond brooch that had belonged to a student's grandmother to a battered Barbie doll that another student had owned ever since she was a small child. The section in this chapter entitled "Educating Fetishes" will help you to incorporate favorite objects from your own life into your use of the fetishes.

PERSONAL JOURNAL WORK

Most people find it helpful to record their work with fetishes in a journal. I use a blank book or a spiral-bound notebook, both of which are available in most office supply stores and bookstores. This record can become a rich source of self-knowledge, allowing you to trace your progress in resolving key issues and to become more aware of the role that your perceptions play in your life.

RELAXATION AND MENTAL PREPARATION

Being in a deeply relaxed state when you work with your fetishes greatly enhances and deepens the process. You may already have your own system of relaxation or meditation. If you don't, I have included in this chapter a relaxation exercise that many people have found easy and effective. It can be done at your desk at work, on a bus or train, or in the privacy of your own room.

THE CARE AND FEEDING OF FETISHES

The Zunis felt it important to respect, honor, and care for the fetishes that were in their possession. They believed that if one did not take care of them, they would cease to be useful to their owner. For this reason, as we've noted in the previous chapter, fetishes were usually kept in a fetish jar (see the illustration) or in a leather pouch. Many of the more powerful fetish sets were kept hidden in a carefully guarded place and were brought out only when they were to be used for consultation or healing.

Although it is not the traditional Zuni way, I keep most of my own fetishes on a shelf in my office. From time to time during a given working day, I may go several times to the shelf and consult with them. I have a healthy respect for rituals that acknowledge the mysteries of life, since they remind us that we humans are not the final authority, so I keep a small bowl nearby filled with cornmeal, and I ritualistically feed the fetishes each time I wish to consult with them.

While following a set ritual can be helpful when you first begin to work with the fetishes, you will probably develop your own style of working with them over time. The following three elements, however, were included in most of the Zuni rituals that used fetishes:

Feeding—An offering of fresh cornmeal is made. Originally, this offering was made at least once a day and at any time the fetish was consulted. Fresh meal was always offered, and the previous offering was swept away and discarded.

Breathing—Breath is the equivalent of the living spirit. Thus, when one wishes to ask a fetish for help, the person holds the fetish's nose to his or her own lips, breathes over the fetish, and then breathes in its breath or spirit.

Prayers—When a prey fetish was used for a hunt, the hunter of-fered a prayer and planted a plumed arrow shaft (or prayer stick) in the ground to honor the fetish and mark the place where the prayer was offered.

RELAXATION AND CENTERING

As taught in most Eastern traditions, meditation and centering are ways of focusing on the present, of placing ourselves in the flow of the Tao. Modern consciousness research, using electroencephalo-graphs to measure impulses in the nervous system, shows that in deep meditative states our brain waves become increasingly quiet. In the active waking state, called beta, the waves fluctuate at thirteen to twenty-six cycles per second; in the deep meditative state, called theta, the fluctuations decrease to between one and four cycles per second.

In the meditative state, muscles throughout the body are relaxed, the mind is at ease, and a harmony exists both physiologically and psychologically that causes us to experience a sense of well-being. At this point, the human consciousness functions in a way that is very different from its active state. The two hemispheres of the brain are balanced, intuition and reason at rest, and we begin to discover men-tal resources we were not aware we had; we dream or "envision" ma-terial that takes us outside everyday consciousness into what is ordinarily understood as the spiritual realm.

The spiritual reality that people often experience in deeply relaxed consciousness states is life stripped of the personal perceptions and interpretations that we ordinarily project onto the world around us. As we quiet that portion of the brain where individualized percep-tions are formed and held, we begin to see another reality. We see past our highly individualized beliefs and feelings to a more universal knowledge that is applicable to all. The insights we bring back from this state cannot usually be verbalized. Attempts to verbalize them usually leave us frustrated; the inability to capture these insights in words sometimes causes people to feel that what they experienced was illusory or "unreal," when in fact they are accessing truths that are timeless and universal.

The richest insights you will receive from the fetishes are those experienced in the meditative state, stripped of the everyday perceptions that you or others project onto the world. The process I describe for working with these insights helps you translate them back into everyday terms, terms that are practical and easy to employ for resolving specific issues in your life.

If you already have your own meditation or centering techniques, you can skip this section. For those of you who wish to use the exercises presented here, I recommend that you tape-record the following. Then you can play the instructions back to yourself, leaving you free to be completely relaxed and centered. Recording the instructions may take a little experimentation on your part, for you need to record them at a pace that you can follow comfortably.

After you have done these exercises half a dozen times, you will probably find that you no longer need to be so systematic about them. You will be able to take a few deep breaths, close your eyes, and go immediately into a relaxed state. Most people find that they can eventually do this at their desks at work, in line at the supermarket, or even on the bus commuting to or from work.

A word of caution here: don't do these exercises in your car. I had one student who played the exercise tape on his car stereo while stuck in freeway traffic. During the five-minute traffic jam, he went into a deep meditative state, only to be jarred into wakefulness by a chorus of blaring horns announcing that traffic was moving again! There are indeed times when we need to stay focused on the external world, rather than turning inward, as the following exercise teaches you to do.

RELAXATION AND CENTERING EXERCISES

Part I: Relaxation

Give yourself permission to take five or ten minutes to relax deeply, with no interruptions or distractions. Choose a place to do this exercise and a time of day when this will be possible.

▲ Loosen any tight clothing.

▲ Sit in an alert, upright position, hands gently lying in your lap with your palms open.

▲ Let your shoulders be loose and relaxed.

▲ Relax your feet, allowing the entire soles to make contact with the earth (or floor).

▲ Open your mouth wide. Yawn, or pretend you are yawning.

▲ Let the areas around your eyes be relaxed. Let your forehead be loose. Let the areas around your nose and mouth be relaxed.

▲ If ideas or feelings enter your mind at this time, pretend they are a telephone ringing in a neighbor's house. You acknowledge that "someone is calling," but you do not need to answer.
(Note: I find that learning *not* to answer your phone when it is ringing helps you recognize that it is not necessary to act upon every thought, feeling, or external signal. As simple and perhaps eccentric as this may seem, learning to ignore a ringing telephone can provide valuable meditation practice.)

▲ Take a deep breath, inhaling gently and slowly, imagining the breath entering your right nostril. Hold the breath for a moment, then slowly exhale, imagining that you are exhaling through your left nostril.

▲ Take a second deep breath, this time imagining your breath coming in through your left nostril and out your right.

▲ Focus your attention on how the breath feels: cooling as it enters your nostrils, perhaps gently agitating the tiny hairs that line your nasal passage, expanding your chest as it fills your lungs, then slightly warming your nostrils as you exhale. You may also wish to visualize the air with a beautiful, vibrant color as it enters and exits your body.

▲ Repeat this breathing pattern until you have done at least four full cycles. A full cycle is one inhalation and one exhalation.

▲ With each cycle, focus your attention on one area of your body:
Be aware of your chest relaxing.
Be aware of your shoulders relaxing.
Be aware of your arms and hands relaxing.
Be aware of your abdomen relaxing.
Be aware of your buttocks relaxing.
Be aware of your legs relaxing.
Be aware of your feet relaxing.

▲ Now let your breathing return to normal. Enjoy this relaxed state.

▲ Let yourself be in this relaxed state while you speak with your fetishes.

For a while, practice this relaxation exercise whenever the opportunity arises. Use it to relax and center yourself whenever you are feeling pressured at work, at home, or in your personal relationships. People who are involved in any form of athletics find that this exercise allows them to be centered and focused; it helps put them in the state of readiness that is necessary for optimal performance.

Part II: Centering

In this exercise you create a sense of feeling grounded, of being secure and oriented in the present. You will find this exercise particularly helpful throughout the day for refocusing on the present when you get off center or out of sync with your surroundings, an experience that is becoming more and more a problem in the pressured, fast-paced world in which so many of us live.

▲ Begin by taking a few deep breaths, exhaling slowly and gently through your nose. When you are preparing to work with the fetishes, complete the deep relaxation exercise first. However, if you are using this exercise for centering during the day when you have other obligations to fulfill, two or three deep breaths is all you will need.

▲ With your eyes closed, imagine that you are sending out thin silver threads or narrow laser beams of light to the eight corners of the room—the four corners of the ceiling and the four corners of the floor. Imagine these threads or beams of light extending from your navel to these eight points. (If the room has a complex configuration, choose eight corners above and four below that are easiest for you to visualize.)

▲ Imagine a silver thread or light beam extending from the base of your spine down through the floor to the center of the earth.

▲ Recall a place in your past experience—perhaps a room in your home, a place you used to go as a child, or a place you have visited on a holiday—where you felt secure, happy, completely at ease with yourself. Imagine a silver thread or beam of light connecting you with that place at this time, extending from your mind's eye (which is at the center of your forehead, between your eyes), your heart, or your navel.

▲ For a few moments, let your attention be focused on the lines you have created between you and the eight corners of the room, the center of the earth, and the place where you feel secure, happy, completely at ease.

▲ Sit and enjoy this experience for twenty to thirty seconds.

▲ When you are ready to do so, take a deep breath, exhale forcefully, and open your eyes.

▲ Look around you and check out your relationship to the four corners of the room and the four corners of the floor.

You will now be ready to begin whatever work you choose to do with your fetishes.

GETTING TO KNOW THE FETISHES: BEGINNING METHOD

The old saying, often attributed to Native Americans, that before one judges another he or she should "walk a mile in that person's moccasins" might well apply to learning how to work with your fetishes. Each fetish has an individual identity. It stands for different ideas, experiences, and universal principles. It offers a different point of view. When we consult with the fetishes, we are forced to look at our own lives, if only for a moment, through different eyes. As we take in these new perspectives, our own inner vision clears because we begin to discover, among other things, that there are ways to look at the world other than those that we create in our minds. The fetishes offer us the opportunity to see our lives in a different light, expanding our vision so that we find it not only easier to solve our problems but also easier to enjoy a spiritually richer life.

It is important to note here that when the Ashiwi began working with fetishes many hundreds of years ago, they lived very closely with animals, and the animals were far more abundant than they are today. The "meanings" for the fetishes came not from books but from observing animals in their natural habitat, day after day, year after year.

The elders observed the animals, the humans, the seasons, the growth of plants, and natural phenomena such as lightning—in short, all of the natural world—far more accurately than any people do today. Their wisdom came from the primary teacher, life itself, not from books or the media, as it often does today.

The instructions and the fetish readings that I provide here are meant to act as a bridge, helping us to connect with primordial sources. They are not intended to replace teachings that might come more directly than this source, but only to point a helpful direction, to offer another way of seeing.

As you introduce yourself to your fetishes, keep in mind that whatever firsthand experience you have regarding the animal you are working with is important. If the information you already have—felt as a strong pull within your heart or mind—contradicts what you read in this book, do not be afraid to favor that firsthand knowledge over what is written here. You may find that these readings help to fill in other aspects of that fetish that you hadn't felt or thought about, but your own experience should be respected.

Begin by getting to know the Guardians of the six Directions—Mountain Lion, Black Bear, White Wolf, Badger, Bald Eagle, and Mole. To do this, put yourself in a deeply relaxed state and study the readings of these six fetishes provided in Chapter Four. If you have a figure for the fetish you are studying, hold it in your hand as you read or put it down in front of you so that you can combine your tactile or visual sense with the more complex intellectual process of reading.

If you don't have an actual fetish for the animal you are studying, focus your attention on the drawings this book provides. At the same time, allow the new insights associated with the animal to mix in your mind with any prior knowledge that you may have of him or her. Let your mind play with the fetishes and with the ideas or insights they evoke. This playtime can include anything you might imagine.

One woman imagined herself walking down the main street of her hometown in Ohio with a full-sized black bear walking beside her. She imagined meeting people she knew and introducing them to the bear. The bear was able to carry on regular conversations. She gave the bear a complete tour of her hometown, showing her the house where she was born, the public school where she attended kindergarten through sixth grade, the places where she had played and shopped.

Another student imagined that he had a Falcon that he could send off ahead of him to business meetings. He imagined this falcon swooping into the room where the meeting was to be held and fanning its wings, a magic ritual that prepared the room for a relaxed and productive meeting.

The most important ingredient of this getting-acquainted stage is letting your imagination run wild. At the same time, be sure to maintain the "character" of the fetish. The easiest way to do this is to return occasionally to the list of qualities that you find at the top of

each fetish reading. Focus on at least three of these qualities, prefer-
ably those that best individualize for you the fetish you have chosen.

ADDING A NEW FETISH

Whenever I introduce a new fetish to my collection, I actually carry
on an inner dialogue with it. I ask it to tell me its name, its origin,
and how it can serve me. I ask it what its own most important lessons
have been. I pause and quietly wait for answers each time, later
recording whatever comes to me. In general, when I "hear" the
voices of the fetishes, I feel as though I am making it all up, like a
novelist who makes up a character for a book or a child who makes
up imaginary playmates.

Feel free to create and embellish on the descriptions I provide of
the fetishes. If you are keeping a journal of this work, make a special
section where you can write down any notes you wish to add about
the fetishes.

You do not need to get to know every fetish, but I highly recommend that you do get to know the guardians of the six Directions
very well. After that you can study the other fetishes described in
Chapter Four, or you can develop your own fetishes, as described in
the next paragraph.

EDUCATING FETISHES

Don't hesitate to introduce into your work a fetish that is not of Zuni
origin. The main requirement for an object to become useful as a
fetish is that it *holds a charge* for you. By this I mean very simply that
you feel strongly attracted to it. This attraction can be aesthetic,
emotional, or spiritual, or it may be associated with some aspect of
your own history. Wherever there is a strong attraction of this kind,
it means that the object has something to teach you about your life.

Hold the object in your hand and focus your attention on it. Then
begin exploring what it means to you. For example, Eden, who attended a workshop I once gave in New York, had a small silver cross

that had belonged to her grandmother. Her grandmother had been very important to her when Eden was growing up. Now, when she held the cross, Eden felt connected with her grandmother again and could easily recall their conversations of long ago. Eden said that holding the cross in her hand when she was feeling sad or depressed was like "turning on a light"; it always helped her to feel her grandmother's guidance.

Sometimes fetishes or power objects come into our lives that seem to have little or no *charge*. They may be attractive, or they may have been given to us as a gift from someone we love, but they still don't have the charge that would make them useful in our lives. This lack of charge is because the object has no history for us. It may be symbolically right for us—for example, we wanted a Black Bear fetish for our collection so we bought one—but it seems to have no power.

I once purchased a Mountain Lion fetish at an Indian crafts store in a very ordinary suburban shopping center. Every time I tried to work with this fetish, I drew a blank. It seemed to have no identity for me. I had a conference with the other fetishes in my collection, who told me that the object had no history, and I would have to provide it with one.

I took the fetish out into the hills and placed it in a tree, where it remained for several weeks. When I went out and retrieved it, it definitely had a charge. When I held it in my hand, I saw the landscape in which I had placed it. I saw it hunting and maintaining that territory, guarding the boundaries.

The education of a fetish can take many forms, of course. You could place it outside, as I did Mountain Lion. Or you can seek out stories and early legends in books that will give you a sense of how that object was perceived by other people or of how it fit into their cosmology or religious ceremonies.

Once the fetish is educated, place it for a while just outside any collection of fetishes you already have. Let it be integrated slowly into the group. Treat it like the new kid on the block whom the others must get to know and trust before they will let it in. Some fetishes may continue to be outsiders. These become solitary talismans, or they may even become part of a second group of fetishes that are merely decorative for you or that have some designated purpose of their own.

USING THE FETISH AS A TALISMAN

In many religious and spiritual practices, we find some form of the talisman used to help devotees maintain their attention on a religious or spiritual concept. Talismans vary from the phallic figure used in Dionysian cults to represent the generative force, to beads for keeping count of prayers, such as the rosary in Catholicism, to good-luck charms, such as the rabbit's foot in American folklore.

The talisman is popularly thought to have magical powers and thus is supposed to bring its owner good luck, prosperity, and protection from evil influences. More formally, the talisman is a symbol, a reminder, a way to help its owner hold in his or her mind an important and usually complex concept.

For example, I have a small fetish of a bear, carved from a beautiful piece of fine turquoise. This fetish was given to me by a close friend at a time in my life when I was very unhappy, feeling burdened by family problems and financial difficulties. My friend presented this fetish to me with his prayers and good wishes that it would help me carry my burden. He told me that I should think of a bear in the wild; before winter, it would seek out the richest foods it could find, building up fat to provide nutrition during its long sleep. Then it would go into hibernation, retreating to a safe place until the cold season had passed.

The idea was that I could pass my burdens on to Turquoise Bear, who was strong enough to hold them without danger to its health. This would allow me to get my mind off what I could not immediately solve and focus instead on what I could do to be productive and creative. In this way, I would not be ignoring or repressing the rest; I would simply be giving them over to a force, or being, who could hold them, with some degree of comfort, until the time came for me to focus constructive attention on them.

The principle of Turquoise Bear is a little like the serenity prayer often quoted in twelve-step programs: "God grant me the serenity to accept the things I cannot change, the courage to change the things I can, and the wisdom to know the difference."

Turquoise Bear embodies many other concepts for me as well; for example, he reminds me of the need to forgive myself and others for our human limitations, which are so often the source of conflict and reduced self-esteem in our lives.

When I am feeling burdened, I take Turquoise Bear in my hand and hold it while meditating. I focus my attention on the fetish itself, remembering all that it symbolizes and embodies for me. As I do so, the various concepts and techniques I have learned over the years for dealing with difficult times come to the fore, allowing me to employ them in helping me make choices about how best to use my time and energy.

When working with the fetish in this way, I prefer to think of the object not as possessing power in itself but as evoking powers that I myself possess. I prefer to think of fetishes getting their power through the power we project to them. Remember when working with a fetish in this way that unless you had experienced and actually exercised the power yourself, at some point in your life, you could not project that power to the object.

If you do not presently have a fetish that would work for you as a talisman, you can choose one from the descriptions of the fetishes I provide in Chapter Four. You can further develop its symbolic powers by holding it in your hand and recalling moments in your life when you experienced the attribute that you wish it to represent for you. For example, a runner who wants a fetish for psyching herself up before an athletic competition might choose a deer. The deer is swift, graceful, and profoundly in touch with its body. She might hold such a fetish in her hand and recall those times when she was performing at optimal levels, literally bathing the object with those images and feelings. Later, as she holds the fetish in her hand before an important run, it will trigger those memories, complete with many of the neuromuscular responses that accompanied them and that are so important in the psyching-up process.

Similar techniques can, of course, be employed for "programming" a talisman for virtually any purpose. It was Cushing's belief that within the Zuni mythology he could eventually find what Mary Austen called "profoundly mystical prototypes for every essential motion of man's soul."[3] The Zuni fetishes represent a wide range of these prototypes from which we might choose. While any single fetish may not provide us with all the physical, emotional, and spiritual attributes we desire, each fetish's traditional associations do offer a good place to start. The programming of additional associations then becomes a highly individualized matter, for they are brought to a particular fetish by its owner.

As with every use of the fetishes, continued practice is essential in order to build familiarity with the object, the attributes you wish it to represent, and the process itself. When you are just beginning, try to spend at least twenty minutes with the fetish or talisman at least four times a week. The more you invest in the practice, the more useful and powerful it will become for you, eventually tapping into personal resources that will surprise you.

BASIC PRINCIPLES FOR CONSULTING FETISHES

The process for accessing information with the help of your fetishes and then translating these insights into practical terms consists of eight steps. Frame your question carefully, as the instructions describe. Then ask one or more of your fetishes for an answer. Hold the fetish in your hand, or picture it in your mind's eye. Starting with what you already know about the fetish—which you have learned by studying the descriptions I provide in Chapter Four—try to imagine how that animal would answer you.

In the beginning, the answers you get are probably going to seem "made up" to you. They will seem to be simply derived from the descriptions of the fetishes, which you have studied. That's okay. That is how it is supposed to work. As you progress, expect surprising insights and expect the fetishes to take on lives of their own only after you have worked with them on several real-life issues.

The Consulting Process in Action

1. Describe the problem. State the problem or describe the issue you wish to resolve. Do this in very personal terms, focusing on how it affects you emotionally.

> *Joan, who was employed as a mortgage broker at a large bank, described her problem in the following way: "I'm not at all happy with my present job. I feel like I'm just wasting my life and not using my potential."*

After stating the question, wait for your attention to focus on one fetish or another. If you do not feel naturally attracted to one, choose one arbitrarily. Think about the description of that fetish. Using that material, imagine how he or she might respond to your question.

> *Joan addressed her problem to Mountain Lion. She recorded the following as her (Joan's Mountain Lion was a female) reply: "You are unhappy because in your present position you are doing what everyone wants you to do. It's as if other people are always encroaching on your territory. The territory you work in is not a territory you'll ever feel comfortable in. It's not who you are."*

Note how the theme of territorialism reflects the description of Mountain Lion. Joan commented that she felt Mountain Lion's insights were ones she would have come to on her own. However, she also felt this first step was helpful since it gave her a framework for clarifying her own thoughts and bringing them fully to consciousness.

2. Describe a positive outcome. Our perception that a problem exists implies that somewhere in our consciousness we sense that things could be better. Somewhere, hidden within us, is a positive vision of how our lives should be. The purpose of this step is to bring that vision into the light and articulate it as clearly as you can.

> *Joan said, "I want to be able to get up in the morning dying to get to work because I love what I do so much. I'd get to work, people would*

*greet me in a friendly way, and I'd feel that I was really being re-
spected for my abilities and liked for who I really am. Being myself
would please everyone and allow me to get the job done perfectly."*

*This time she imagined Bald Eagle and Black Bear speaking to her.
Black Bear said, "It's time you came out of hibernation and let people
know who you are." Bald Eagle, flying overhead, told her, "You can
give wings to your spirit. You've let your spirit die in your work.
You're staying on there just for the paycheck, but it's just miserable because there's just no life in what you have to do."*

3. Describe the roots of your present problem. Much of the time,
problems we are facing are held in place not simply by present fears
but by lessons from the past that have told us it is risky, impractical,
or simply impossible to do anything differently. We release ourselves
from these beliefs by reaching back into our personal histories and
shining a brilliant light on these fears.

*Joan said, "Any time I imagine leaving my job, I hear my mother's
voice telling me, 'Hold onto what you've got. You don't get anything
without making some personal sacrifices.'"*

*Again, Joan found herself turning to Mountain Lion. This time
the fetish's response surprised her. Mountain Lion said, "Leave your
mother's territory and find your own." Joan interpreted this as meaning that she was allowing herself to be limited by her mother's fears.
She reminded herself that her mother, after all, had been a very inse-
cure person.*

4. Describe what you'd be losing if you changed. Most of the
time there is something, even in the most difficult situations, that we
would like to keep, though we definitely want to change the rest.
However, keeping that one benefit—and be warned, we often hide it
from ourselves—also has a way of keeping us stuck with the things
we want to change.

For example, a friend of mine has two children, a boy and a girl
two years apart. The boy, who is the younger one, often goads the

older girl into hitting him, upon which his mournful cries immediately bring his parents to his defense. At the price of a few minor bruises, he gains the privilege of seeing his older sister punished. This gives him a tremendous feeling of power. When the parents finally caught onto the game and stopped punishing the girl for hitting her brother, the younger boy was furious. He no longer had a way of getting his older sister in trouble. He had to find a new way to experience a sense of power over her.

> *Joan turned to Badger. Her impression of Badger was that he was very stubborn and narrow-minded. Even so, she felt a certain fondness for this animal, for she felt he had a "rascally" quality that she found humorous. In a way, he reminded her of some of her own worst traits, some of which were carryovers over from her childhood. People told her, for example, that when she got angry at her friends or coworkers, she often shot off her mouth, saying things she later regretted. Then she would clam up, refusing to listen to anybody until she had gotten over her anger. Those, she told herself, were her Badger traits, traits which she considered masculine.*
>
> *As she turned her attention to Badger and asked for help in identifying what she must give up, the answer she got surprised her. Badger said, "There's a part of you that actually enjoys getting outraged by the things that happen at your present job. If you had a job you really loved, you'd have to give that up." As surprising as this insight was, Joan knew that it was true, and she immediately started telling herself, "I really am ready to give this up in my life."*

5. Describe how the present circumstances would work out in light of what you have learned so far. For a moment, pretend that you have only to create a mental image of the perfect outcome and you will instantly have it. If there is no way you can fail, what occurs? This can be one of the most challenging of the first five questions because it asks us to define exactly what we want. We are forced to stop focusing on what we *don't* want—that is, on the issues that are the source of our complaints—and focus instead on what we do want.

Joan carefully considered all six fetishes. She tried to imagine what each one of them might say, how they might help her define what it was she really wanted. White Wolf was the first to speak to her. "You have a wonderful knack for supervising others," he said, "yet you have never been in a job where these skills were used. That is one aspect you should seek in a new job."

She then felt that Black Bear wanted to encourage her, to tell her that in a supervisory capacity she would be able to exercise her greatest skills and potential and thus find her greatest satisfaction.

Joan was enjoying this step of the process so much that she ended up talking with each fetish at length, just to see what she could discover about herself. In the end, she had a clear picture of what the real problems were and how solutions could be found.

6. What is your greatest discovery so far? This is a reflective question, asking you to summarize and focus on what the fetishes have helped you to uncover.

Joan said that her greatest discovery was actually twofold: first, that there was a part of her that would rather complain than change, and second, that her deepest satisfaction could be found in seeking employment where her supervisory capabilities were more in evidence.

In this and the next two steps, it is not necessary to speak with the fetishes. Many people do, however, because they find the fetishes can help them clarify their own thoughts and feelings.

7. What is an immediate action you can take to bring about the changes you have identified? Look for something you can do in the next few moments that would be a first step toward making the changes you desire. This can be anything from changing the way you think about the problem, to making a phone call to a friend or business associate, to driving the first nail that begins a major construction project. Whatever you choose, make certain that it is something you can do and complete in the next few moments.

SAMPLE JOURNAL PAGE

1. **Describe the problem.** State the problem or describe the issue you wish to resolve.

2. **Describe an ideal outcome.** Bring the vision of your ideal outcome to light by articulating it as clearly as you can.

3. **Describe the roots of your present problem.** Release yourself from past beliefs or fears by reaching back into your personal history and shining a brilliant light on them.

4. **Describe what you'd be losing if you changed.** Identify the benefits, or secondary gains, of keeping things the way they presently are.

5. **Describe how the present circumstances would work out in light of what you have learned so far.** Create a mental image of the perfect outcome if you could have things exactly as you want.

6. **What is your greatest discovery so far?** Summarize what the fetishes have helped you to uncover.

7. **What is an immediate action you can take to bring about the changes you've identified?** Decide on something you can do in the next few moments that would be a first step toward making the changes you desire.

8. **Describe your long-term goal in bringing about a resolution to this issue.** State your long-term goals so that you can track your progress in achieving significant changes in your life.

8. Describe your long-term goal in bringing about a resolution to this issue. Not every question, or issue, will require you to complete this step of the process. For example, if you were deciding whether or not to go away for the weekend, it would be very unlikely that a long-term goal would be involved. A long-term goal would be involved, however, if you were making a decision to go into business for yourself.

If you are recording your work with the fetishes in a journal, you will find that your statements of long-term goals can help you track your progress whenever you are working on significant change in your life.

USING THE MEDICINE WHEEL

In nearly every early culture throughout the world, there is some variation of what we call the "medicine wheel." Often these are large circles marked out by rocks in the landscape. Usually, the four directions are indicated by larger rocks, thus forming the equivalent of the four quadrants of the compass. The center, or hub, of the medicine wheel is often indicated by a second, inner circle formed of smaller rocks.

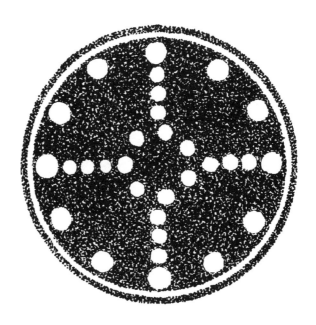

Explanations for the medicine wheel vary greatly from one culture to another, but it generally has symbolic significance, and around these formations many important ceremonies occur.

The Zuni equivalent of the medicine wheel is suggested by the six major prey fetishes: Mountain Lion, White Wolf, Badger, Black Bear, Mole, and Eagle. With these having been assigned the guardianship of the Six Regions of the world, we have a microcosm of the macrocosm, or a conceptual model of the entire universe. Likewise, the six fetishes, each with its own set of qualities and its own place in the cosmology and religion of the tribe, are, in Mary Austen's terms, "mystical prototypes" of the external forces that affect our lives as well as of the various inner drives that move us.

As we have learned, the Zunis believed that it was their destiny to seek the Middle Place and that when they at last found it, they would prosper, multiply, and be happy. The Six Directions—North, South, East, West, Above, and Below—define where the middle can be found.

If one is to read this symbolically, the middle that the Zunis sought is similar to the Tao in ancient Chinese philosophy—that is, it is not a geographic location so much as a spiritual concept. The Middle exists for us whenever we are completely at one with the present and with the common spirit uniting us all. It is that which is timeless and eternal. The Tao, according to Lao-tzu, is also a Middle Place:

> *Meet it and you will not see its head.*
> *Follow it and you will not see its back.*[4]

Thus, to consult with the fetishes representing the Guardians of the Six Directions is to learn how to stand at the Middle, that is, to be completely in the here and now, in the Tao.

There is also an interesting and instructive parallel between the Zuni concept of the Middle Place and the Buddhist "Middle Path," that is, the path "which leads to wisdom, which conduces to calm, to knowledge . . . to Nirvana."[5] On this Path, we give our lives to the eightfold Path, namely: Right Belief, Right Aspiration, Right Speech, Right Conduct, Right Means of Livelihood, Right Endeavor, Right Memory, Right Meditation."[6]

From the Middle, guided by any interpretation of what this means for us, we can reflect on our lives and any problems we might be facing by seeking the perspectives of each of the six regions. At the Middle, we are in a position to encounter the universal forces that determine the course of our lives. The following abbreviated interpretations of the symbolism of the Middle will help clarify this:

At the Middle, we become aware of north and south. These represent the energetic coordinates of the planet and therefore of our lives. Astronomers tell us that the planet spinning on its north-south pole sets up a magnetic field that flows from south to north, then out into a space in a butterfly shape that envelops the entire planet. This magnetic field allows us to maintain our balanced and harmonious relationship with all other celestial bodies and with the universal energy that sustains the whole.

It is at the middle of the north-south coordinates that we encounter the energetic matrix of the earth. Within each cell of our bodies, we also find magnetic poles like the north and south poles of the earth, with a butterfly-shaped field flowing out and around each one; thus, each cell is connected energetically with all the things of the earth as well as with the earth herself and with the whole.

In traditional Zuni thought, the earth was perceived as our Mother. Legend has it that we are products of a union between Mother Earth and Father Sky, and it is out of Mother Earth's womb that we are born. Thus, to find the Middle is to be in perfect harmony with our Mother, who gave us life in our present form. This harmony consists, on the physical plane, of a kind of magnetic balance between all beings of the earth and the earth itself, if we're speaking in purely practical terms, or as spiritual harmony, if we're speaking in terms of a cosmology.

Two other universal forces encountered at the middle are the east-west coordinates. As the legends of Poshaiankia express it, the east is the direction from which the new day comes, while the west is where the day goes at night. Not only is the diurnal cycle described here but also implied are the cycles of all beginnings and endings, of birth and death, as well as the human concepts of time. At the middle, we perceive not only genesis and exodus (the arrival and the departure) but we also see these as part of a cycle, expressions of a larger universal pattern.

Finally, there are the universal forces of above and below. Here we encounter heaven and earth, the infinite spiritual aspects as well as the finite and time-bound aspects of our lives. While above and below can refer to physical coordinates—literally the sky above us and the earth under our feet—these directions can also refer to metaphysical concepts. For example, below can refer to our inner world—the world of dreams, hidden feelings, and the shadow self. Above can refer to the spiritual world—those aspects of ourselves that identify us as part of a force greater than we are.

When consulting the fetishes that stand for the six regions, our goal first and foremost is to be as much in the present, as much in the middle—in the Tao—as we can possibly be. Once this is accomplished, we can go on to consult the fetishes who, as we are beginning to see, are reference points for universal truths that apply to virtually every major issue in our lives.

PLACING YOURSELF AT THE WHEEL

To form a medicine wheel with the prey fetishes, we face north and place our chosen figures on the ground, or floor, in front of us, much as the hunter in the story at the beginning of this chapter did. Mountain Lion marks the North Region or quadrant; Badger, the South; Black Bear, the West; and White Wolf, the East. I prefer to place Eagle, representing the Upper Regions, to the right of the wheel, close to White Wolf, since both suggest spiritual forces—the air, or upper regions, and the East, or beginnings. I place Mole, the Guardian of the lower regions, to the South, since for me this direction suggests earthbound, basic drives.

One need not have all the fetishes available in order to form a medicine wheel. Simply envision any of the missing fetishes in your mind's eye.

The following interpretations, which assign different meanings to the six regions, or directions, of the medicine wheel, are not necessarily authentic to the Zunis. The meanings have been extrapolated from the reading of stories, myths, and other fragments of the cosmology that have been published in various sources. Even the traditionalist should allow some creative license, however, since individual interpretation of privately owned fetish collections—particularly those of healers—has apparently been respected throughout history.

In the medicine wheel that I use, all fetishes face to the center of the circle, as if giving attention to the Middle. As I have already noted, I believe that the middle has a metaphysical meaning, suggesting a state of being in harmony with the natural forces, focused on the here and now, fully present with ourselves and those around us. The arrangement of the medicine wheel, with the six prey fetishes facing inward, reminds me of the importance of this focus, and after working with the wheel in this way over a period of time one is guided to focus his/her own attention in this way.

Mountain Lion, Guardian of the North, represents the highest form of knowledge to which humans may aspire: wisdom. This knowledge comes about through an integration of the experiences of this lifetime—all the successes and failures, joys and sorrows, fulfillments and disappointments we experience—with the universal and spiritual knowledge that is a part of everyone's life—such as an acceptance of the cycles of life and death, as well as of the mysteries of form and formlessness, and the ability to grasp the existence of forces greater than ourselves that are eternal rather than finite like our own short lives here on earth. To sit at the North is to have wisdom, to have integrated at least some of our individual experiences, our trials, tribulations, victories, and joys, with the greater universal knowledge.

White Wolf, Guardian of the East, suggests illumination, our quest for higher knowledge rather than our possession of it. The East, let us remember, is the place of new beginnings, the start of every new day. In most religions, the East is the direction from which come the great teachers, the "enlightened" ones put here to teach us.

To sit at the East is to seek higher knowledge and occasionally to teach; as we learn in many spiritual traditions, the teacher is ordinarily one who is still learning.

Badger, Guardian of the South, suggests many of the basic, aggressive drives of human life. Driven by the needs of the ego and the physical body, Badger can be so caught up in the satisfaction of such drives—sexuality, hunger, jealousy, acquisitiveness, fear, competitiveness, judgment of self and others, vengeance—that it wantonly destroys. The wanton destruction of others, whether through the injury of another's feelings or through actual physical harm, is always shortsighted and narrow, since it ignores the fact that to injure anything within the universal oneness is to injure oneself. To sit at the south is to acknowledge that in some respect we are all presently caught up in the basic human drives.

Black Bear, Guardian of the West, signifies personal strength and introspection, the ability to go inward, examine oneself, and seek some resolve about the often contradictory nature of our spiritual selves and our basic human drives. It is through the strengths represented by Black Bear that we ultimately come to wisdom. To sit at the West is to be introspective, that is, to look at ourselves and, facing East, recognize that even the darkest recesses of our psyches can be illuminated with the light of spiritual understanding.

Eagle, Guardian of the Upper Regions, signifies our ability to pursue the heights. To fly like an eagle is to master the twin forces of Mother Earth and Father Sky, gaining the perspective of a very large picture. To ride the wings of the eagle is to momentarily escape our human cares and play in the currents created by Earth and Sky.

Mole, Guardian of the Lower Regions, burrows within. Though blind to all but a rudimentary sense of light and dark, it is acutely sensitive to the vibrations, smells, tastes, sounds, and feelings (tactile) of the inner earth forces. To bore into the earth with the Mole is to touch the deep forces from which emanate the lives of plants—herbs, natural medicines, staples such as corn and grains, and so on—and to know the source of underground rivers, the chemistry of minerals, and the chemistry of decay that enriches the feeding plants and other beings of the soil. To stand with Mole is to be close to the heart of Mother Earth.

While most of us tend to want to assign a hierarchy of values to the various fetishes and their qualities, the truth is that each is necessary to form the medicine wheel, and the wheel, with its six directions, represents the whole. Thus, when brought together at the medicine wheel, all are equal and inseparable.

PUTTING IT TOGETHER

How, then, do we make use of the wheel?

The first step is simply to study and note certain things. For example, note that each of the animals, facing toward the center of the wheel, also faces its opposite. The Badger, driven by ego and basic physical needs, faces Mountain Lion, or wisdom, the integration of these needs with a knowledge that transcends a single individual's lifespan. This reminds us that what we perceive from the Badger mind is only a narrow band of knowing. Mountain Lion, in turn, faces Badger, who keeps him focused on the fact that regardless of our higher wisdom, there are the realities of human existence that must not be ignored; these, too, are part of the puzzle given us to ponder.

Black Bear, the introspective, faces east, reminded that in the effort to understand and integrate our life experiences, we are not without the aid of illumination and light.

White Wolf, facing west, is reminded that part of our quest is the contemplation of our inner selves, the search for self-understanding, and a liberation from the Badger mind that otherwise blocks us from making use of the light.

Eagle, meanwhile, is able to see, at least from a distance, through the eyes of any figure in the wheel. Mole has a similar perspective, though his is that of sensing the energies in his own special ways, rather than through the "vision" of his "eyes," which see no light.

At any time, you can add prey fetishes to the wheel. For example, you might wish to bring in Coyote, placing him or her in whatever position that you intuitively sense.

In a deeply relaxed or meditative state, let your mind wander freely over the wheel, noting any relationships or insights that arise as you do. When you are ready, you may wish to bring a problem or question to the "conference" of advisers you have now established within the wheel.

Bringing Your Issue to the Wheel

Think about the wheel and the qualities that are represented in the six positions, and ask yourself where you would place yourself at this time. Here is an example:

Ruth was deeply distressed about her teenage son, who had recently been arrested by the local police for having beer in his car after a concert. She felt that she had failed the boy as a mother. She also felt that with the police involved, the whole matter had been taken out of her control. She felt angry toward her son, impotent where the police were concerned, and downright vengeful toward the boy's father who she believed had not spent enough time with him. At the same time she was doing a lot of soul-searching, looking for ways that she might change her own way of relating to the boy.

Ruth studied the medicine wheel and placed herself in the southwest quadrant, halfway between Badger and Black Bear. She instantly acknowledged that she felt completely caught up in her Badger mind at the moment, but she was also reminded that across the way slightly to her left was Mountain Lion, promising that there was a way to break free of her present dilemma and come to a deeper understanding.

As she was first laying out the medicine wheel, she had done something she didn't usually do. She had placed Coyote halfway between Mountain Lion and White Wolf. Though she hadn't done it consciously, she now realized that she was looking at this figure directly across the center of the wheel. She asked Coyote what this could mean, waiting with a still mind for an answer. Finally, she remembered stories of Coyote as a trickster and a fool, even at times an illusionist. She decided that what this meant was that she should not allow herself to be devastated by this incident with her son. Though it was serious enough, she was somehow bringing to it a sense of gravity it did not deserve. Her own "coyote mind" was making the event out to be much worse than it had to be.

Next she considered her proximity to Black Bear. Though she tended to be an introspective person anyway, she also knew that too much self-reflection quickly dragged her into depression and despair. Looking to her right, she saw White Wolf, offering illumination, a light in the darkness.

In her mind, she asked each fetish in turn for advice and strength, for a way of seeing the present problem in a new light, one that would provide her with a new, more constructive path to follow. Each time she asked a question of one of the fetishes, she focused on that fetish's particular strengths and allowed its perspective and its insights to bubble to the surface.

How would she use the perspective of Badger? To remind her that she was only human and would be prone to the devastating anger and impotence that she was feeling. At the same time, she was reminded that through Mountain Lion there was hope that one day she might actually benefit from this difficult lesson. During her entire reading she was aware of Eagle, hovering overhead, like an all-seeing guardian, protecting her and reminding her not to get trapped by her own fear.

Coyote reminded her not to be tricked by her own mind and her tendency to exaggerate problems when she was feeling overwhelmed by them.

At last she came to Mole. Here she was reminded that when problems became particularly intense in her life, she nearly always found peace in her garden. This was perhaps the best insight of all. That same evening she began working with the dirt, planting a new bed of flowers, an experience that allowed her to feel balanced and whole; Mole's advice was tremendously empowering to her.

We see from Ruth's example that the principles of using the medicine wheel are really quite simple, consisting largely of asking questions, looking with the "mind's eye" and then listening with the "third ear" for answers. Focusing on the various principles and attributes characterized by the different fetishes is an expanding experience, helping us to escape the obstacles and blocks we throw in our own paths.

It can be helpful, as you work with the fetishes in this way, to choose a figure that best represents you at the time you come to the wheel to seek help. Are you feeling Badgerlike, Coyotelike, Bearlike, or what? Be honest about this. For a moment you might want to hold in your hand the fetish that best represents you. Let yourself experience what it really means to you to act as this creature. Then seek balance by asking for the council of other fetishes that possess values that seem to bring you strength, insight, and a picture of a more peaceful and constructive path you can follow.

As you work with the fetishes at the medicine wheel, handle them. Pick them up, close your eyes, breathe their "spirit," and envision them as they might be in real life. Imagine their *spirit* or essence coming into you, the way I described a few pages back. Let your communication with the fetish occur at different levels—mental, emotional, spiritual, and physical. Some people feel themselves as becoming a bear, eagle, and so on, assuming that being's complete identity for a moment. To do these things is to make full use of the fetishes, not limiting yourself to the intellectual insights that are, incidentally, just as important.

In order to get the most from the medicine wheel, work with it on a regular basis. The wheel provides a way of working through problems unlike any other we are taught in modern society. It can seem quite daunting at first, particularly as you study the meanings of the different directions or regions and their Guardian Fetishes. But you will also discover that, like so many other things, *it is much easier to do than to say.* Practice itself touches the process better than all the words in the world will ever do.

THE FETISH CONFERENCE

The last method for using the fetishes is the conference. The main difference between this method and that of the medicine wheel is that here you need not form the wheel itself. Instead, you simply choose two or more fetishes with which to consult. Make your selection either from the list provided in Chapter Four or by following your own intuition.

Place your selections before you and play freely with their positionings. For example, you might find that you want to place Coyote next to Mole. In nature, this proximity might be disastrous for the Mole. But here among the fetishes, where no one is eaten, it might result in a surprising dialogue.

As you consult with the fetishes in this way, explore the different relationships between figures that you either deliberately or accidentally establish. Is there something to be learned in the odd relationship you have set up between Mole and Coyote?

I remember once being stuck on a creative problem in a book I was writing. There was a long passage that I was very fond of but was not coming together with the rest of the book. As I chose fetishes for a conference, doing so in a somewhat careless manner, I noticed that I had placed a small amethyst frog that I own at the Falcon's feet. In fact, Falcon appeared to be eyeing the Frog hungrily, contemplating a tasty treat.

I struggled for just a few moments before realizing that the way to get past this particular writing block was as simple as it should have been self-evident. Let the Falcon eat the Frog! It was suddenly clear that the wonderful passage of which I was so fond really didn't belong in that book. It was the Frog that had to be sacrificed to the larger cause. The Falcon found it a tasty morsel indeed!

OFFERING PRAYERS OF GRATITUDE

Many of the traditional Zuni hunting stories are intended to instruct young hunters in the use of prayers. In one, the young man begins his hunt by planting a prayer stick and thanking the gods of the hunt for the game he is about to bag. His teacher, however, corrects him, saying, "Don't give thanks for what you haven't yet received. The gods, like humans, hate to be indebted."

Other stories warn against telling the gods what to do or presuming that we, mere mortals, can judge or know how to "correct" an error or oversight on the part of the gods. What, then, is the content of one's prayers? Very simply, prayer is a way to seek a release from our own limits and express gratitude.

The hunter or the healer always begins any ritual by offering prayers to the six regions or directions. At the least these should include the following:

An expression of gratitude for Mother Earth, from whose womb we came and from whose breast we are nurtured.

An expression of gratitude to Father Sky, who holds Grandfather Sun, the source of all life energy.

An expression of gratitude for the East, for giving us the sunrise of each new day and from whom we receive every new beginning.

An expression of gratitude for the West, home of the great ocean, for giving us the sunset of each day and for providing endings, the night sky, and the beings who belong to the night.

An expression of gratitude for the North, for giving us the white light of wisdom and peace.

An expression of gratitude for the South, for giving us the human passions through which we seek our place in this life and through which we are moved to seek a wisdom beyond ourselves.

In addition, prayers of gratitude should be offered to each fetish before and after calling upon it for assistance. As you do so, keep in mind that you are giving gratitude not for the object itself but for the spirit or essence that the object represents.

In our prayers, we need to let the gods know of our needs. According to the traditional teachers, these needs are to be stated simply, with no demands made. Certainly one does not order the gods around! Thus, the hunter might say, "My family and I hunger for the flesh of the deer," or "We no longer have grain to feed our cattle." The prayer might proceed, "I pray for your guidance in my hunt, that I might find the trail easy and have good fortune in finding the deer," or "I pray that I might hear and have the wisdom to follow your guidance in planting my crops."

And finally, gratitude must be offered for whatever we receive, whether it seems to be the direct result of our own efforts or the effortless answer to a prayer. Both are, after all, the same—gifts from a source beyond ourselves. Many great teachers also instruct us to give thanks for those we see as our enemies, since it is often through adversity that we ultimately realize our greatest growth.

MOVING FORWARD

With all of this information in mind, you are now ready to become better acquainted with the fetishes and their meanings. I suggest that you scan all the readings in Chapter Four briefly, allowing yourself extra time to study those that particularly interest you.

If you don't yet own any fetishes, the descriptions that follow can be particularly helpful for choosing one or more as the first ones to work with. And if you don't at this time wish to buy the actual fetishes, the pictures provided with these descriptions can serve you almost as well as the real thing—particularly if you can hold them in your mind's eye so that they seem quite real to you.

HOW TO USE
THE FETISH READINGS

It naturally follows from the Zuni's philosophy of life, that his worship,
while directed to the more mysterious and remote powers of nature, or,
as he regards them, existences, should relate more especially to the animals;
that, in fact, the animals, as more nearly related to himself than are these
existences, more nearly related to these existences than to himself,
should be frequently made to serve as mediators between them and him.

FRANK HAMILTON CUSHING[1]

THE MORE WE LEARN about the Zuni fetish and the role it plays in the Ashiwi people's spiritual practices, the more it becomes obvious that to treat these objects only as objects misses the point and borders on the irreverent. Just as the devout Christian or Jew or Muslim or Buddhist treats holy objects in a much more reverent way than they treat objects such as ordinary kitchen utensils or a piece of recently purchased jewelry, so the Ashiwi treat their fetishes with a reverence that far exceeds its objective value.

We should remember that within the framework of the whole Zuni cosmology, there is ultimately only one Spirit that permeates all. Anything in the physical world—whether an animal, a human, a rock, or a fetish—is simply another way in which this spirit manifests itself. To show our respect for this belief, we address everything we encounter in our lives as a "being"—that is, as having a spiritual reality that needs to be honored and respected.

As a being, each fetish has personal qualities that tend to characterize it. Thus, you will find that the first thing after the name in the fetish readings that follow is a list of qualities that the particular fetish represents. These will help you get acquainted with the fetish as quickly and easily as possible. The list also provides you with a catalogue of qualities for those times when you are seeking a fetish to help you work out a specific problem or to support certain qualities in yourself.

After the list, under the "Legend" heading, I have attempted to re-capture some of the original significance of each fetish as it applies to the early Zuni culture. As much as possible, I have honored the ancient cosmologies, religious beliefs, and legends so that original meanings could at least be traced back for those who wished to link them with the traditional ways.

From these two categories, you will begin to get a feeling for the fetish as a "being"—that is, as something more than an object. You'll find that you will develop this sense even further as you hold the fetish in your hand and carry on a dialogue with it, as described in the previous chapter.

In "Affirmations," the next category of each reading, you'll find something a little different. This section focuses on applications, on how the specific fetish can serve you. The affirmations will be particularly helpful if you wish to use a fetish as a talisman, but they will also help you build your relationships with the fetishes as beings.

Each reading concludes with a section entitled "Areas to Explore." Here I have tried to honor the cycles of life as represented by the Medicine Wheel—particularly the idea that our path to wisdom must include periods of self-examination and introspection. In "Areas to Explore," you will find suggestions for using the fetish as a guide along this path.

SPECIAL ELEMENTS FOR THE GUARDIANS OF THE SIX DIRECTIONS

You will notice that in the first six fetish readings, there are some headings that don't appear in the other readings. This is because the first six fetishes are the Guardian fetishes, assigned by Poshaiankia to guard the six regions. The region to which each of these fetishes has been assigned is given a name, such as "Direction of the Home of the Waters," and each is associated with a specific color. Only the Guardian Fetishes are identified in these ways.

A WORD ABOUT INDIVIDUAL COLOR AND DECORATIONS

Long ago, all fetishes were found objects. The lucky person who found a rock that resembled a coyote, bear, or other animal felt that he or she had indeed been blessed. Such rocks, following the ancient myths, were believed to capture the spirit of the animal they resembled. The finder would immediately bring the object to the proper member of the tribe, usually the Priest of the Prey Brotherhood, along with a flint arrowhead and any desired ornaments, called *thlaa*, for dressing. These ornaments were then fastened by means of either cotton string or a thin leather thong to the back and sides of the fetish, just as one might attach objects carried by a beast of burden.

The *thlaa* might consist of tiny mollusk shells or other pieces of shell from the ocean, feathers (often from an eagle), bits of turquoise, coral, beads of varying materials, black stone fragments or beads, and either made or found objects resembling a snake or bolt of lightning.

The univalves (tiny mollusk shells) were highly valued. They were called *tsuikeinane*, or "heart shells." They were considered the most sacred of all shells.

Depending on the intended use of the fetish (to help in war, hunting, healing, family relationships, or agriculture), the arrowhead had different symbolic meanings. It might refer to the great power of the

Bow and Arrow (rainbow and lightning) of Poshaiankia and thus be associated with the powers of nature or the emblematic "Knife of War" believed to protect warriors from unexpected attacks. Sometimes, in the sacred orders of the warriors, the arrowhead was attached to the underbelly of the fetish; it was then believed to obscure the bearer's tracks and make it impossible for enemies to follow him.

When a piece of bright red coral or other red stone is among the decorations, this signifies the heart of the fetish and helps to make the fetish particularly valuable for the healing arts.

Occasionally, one finds bits of shell attached to a fetish that are cut in the jagged shape of a lightning bolt or a snake. Both the snake and lightning bolt signify the energy that is unleashed when lightning bursts in the heavens; thus, these symbols link the owner to that power. Such an ornament is believed to enhance the inherent power of the fetish.

Eagle feathers were highly prized by the Ashiwi people. Various meanings could be assigned to their attachment on the back of a fetish, but any meaning would have its roots in the belief that the Eagle dominated the Upper Regions.

The color of the decorative beads or stones, as well as the color of the fetish itself, is important, for the color refers to one of the regions originally defined by Poshaiankia. Legend held that each region had a great sea at its center. At the center of the sea was a great mountain peak: Mountain Yellow to the North; Mountain Blue to the West; Mountain Red to the South; Mountain White to the East; Mountain All-color above; and Mountain Black below. Thus, a blue bear would be associated with the West, a yellow bear with the North, and so on.

Make note of any natural markings on your fetish. For example, I have a many-colored Bear of a hard, highly polished granitelike material, which has a snow-white marking on its rump in the shape of a snake basking in the sun. Another, about a half inch in diameter, is carved of opal in a reddish-colored matrix; the opal itself, about a half inch in diameter, providing it with the healing powers of that stone.

The exact symbolism of the ornaments varied from one order or "priesthood" to another. In addition, how one decorated a fetish was often highly individualized, influenced by the owner's private history.

While a person who chooses to strictly follow the traditional way would be wise to learn the symbolic and sacred meanings assigned to these ornaments, others can be content with much looser, more personal interpretations.

DAILY CARE

I'd like to make one final suggestion that if you are planning to use your fetishes in the ways described in this book, give them the care and respect they deserve. I have seen people toss their fetishes carelessly in a desk drawer, among paper clips, stamps, scissors, and rulers, and then wonder why they don't "get anything out of them."

I can assure you that if you treat your fetishes like commonplace paraphernalia, then you will get the equivalent back from them. It is our investment of meaning, care, understanding, and reverence that gives them their power or opens us up to discover it. Treat a family member with this same kind of indifference and you will not "get anything" out of him or her either.

Designate a home for your fetishes. In ancient times, a hunter's set of prey fetishes was always returned to the priest of that order, who kept the set together in either its own large fetish bowl or woven basket. The priest honored them with prayers, ritualistically fed them, and was responsible for their safety. Each year, a great ceremony was held to acknowledge their value to the tribe and to honor them for their service.

Traditionally, an individual would have kept his or her own fetishes in a large fetish jar (see the illustration in Chapter Two), but most people today are probably going to settle for something simpler. You might place them on a piece of buckskin or silk on a safe shelf, for example. If you are primarily interested in using a fetish as a talisman, find a pouch that will hold it in your pocket or that can be hung by a thong around your neck.

As suggested in the previous chapter, you should also consider expressing your respect and your desire to learn more from the fetishes through prayers of gratitude and daily ritual feedings.

CHAPTER FOUR

FETISH READINGS

List of Fetishes

I. *Mountain Lion*

II. *Black Bear*

III. *Badger*

IV. *White Wolf*

V. *Eagle*

VI. *Mole*

VII. *Coyote*

VIII. *Snake*

IX. *Raven*

X. *Falcon*

XI. *Owl*

XII. *Rabbit*

XIII. *Fox*

XIV. *Armadillo*

XV. *Turtle*

XVI. *Frog*

XVII. *Deer (Bison)**

XVIII. *Horse*

XIX. *Mirror Stone*

---

* See note on page 152.

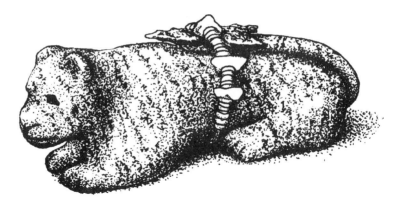

I. MOUNTAIN LION—GUARDIAN OF THE NORTH

Direction of the Swept or Barren Place

▲ *Personal power*
▲ *Territorialism*
▲ *Intuitive ability*
▲ *Steadfastness*
▲ *Bond with Higher Source*
▲ *Resourcefulness*
▲ *Loyalty or dedication*
▲ *Inner spirit*

Color: Yellow

LEGEND

For the Zunis, Mountain Lion was Master Hunter, known for its high intelligence, its knowledge of other animals and life forms, its physical prowess, its strength of will, and its intuitive ability. This animal is highly territorial, clearly understanding its boundaries and limits. It perceives the maintenance of its territory as essential for its individual survival, the survival of its family, and the survival of its species. It also instinctively understands that its role in the great web of life is an integral part of a higher order that it can only begin to comprehend.

Poshaiankia designated Mountain Lion as guardian of the North because of this animal's personal power, superior knowledge, strength of will, and steadfastness.

Poshaiankia assigned Mountain Lion the duty of carrying messages from humans to the higher spirits. Thus, this animal represents the conduit between ourselves and the most powerful spirits in Zuni mythology: Mother Earth, Father Sky, and the Originator of All. Mountain Lion is our spiritual link with all cosmic and natural forces.

When we meditate on Mountain Lion, the things that generally come to mind are personal boundaries or territories, litheness, and power of spirit, especially the spirit within us that is the source of our personal power.

Mountain Lion's resourcefulness as Master Hunter suggests strength and skill in anything having to do with one's livelihood and basic survival needs. Mountain Lion offers assistance when you are seeking to clarify goals, duties, responsibilities, and personal rights that have to do with work, career choices, or relationships. It can encourage your own strength and resourcefulness when you are seeking work, making new connections, and negotiating personal conflicts or differences.

AFFIRMATIONS

Mountain Lion reminds us that it is often our own power of will or volition, the spirit of life that resides in each of us, that gives us the power to act and think and feel, that allows us to go forward to solve our daily problems and actualize the dreams we hold most dear.

If you are feeling down, put Mountain Lion in front of you and allow it to call forth a mental picture of this powerful, lithe creature in the wild. Then draw upon the enlivening spirit this image evokes, letting power, grace, and agility imbue your heart, your mind, and your own spirit.

If you feel your personal boundaries or rights are being violated in any way, bring the image of Mountain Lion to mind. Think of its resolute dedication to patrolling its own boundaries, letting the world know its needs and its perceptions clearly and unequivocally. Allow yourself to have that sense of clarity and single-minded purpose. For a moment, put aside all thoughts of compromise; focus without apology on what it is you want or need. Then go back out into the world with a readiness to negotiate while you remain true to your own beliefs, feelings, and needs. Let the world know who you are and what you expect.

If you are feeling alone, meditate on Mountain Lion to remind you that the illusion of separation you may be experiencing is only that, an illusion. We are each part of a great whole that is much larger than any of us can comprehend. Mountain Lion can help us find once again our links with nature and the cosmos and thus rediscover our oneness, dissolving all our illusions of separation and aloneness. Mountain Lion is there to remind us that we each have an open line to the Creative Source.

AREAS TO EXPLORE

At the top of the list are issues involving personal boundaries. Are you giving too much away, making it difficult or impossible to explore your own inner gifts? Or are you guarding your territory so adamantly that others are fearful of approaching you, making it difficult or impossible for you to receive assistance or affection?

Seek a greater balance between the amount of energy you are putting into material security and pleasure and the energy you are putting into deeper personal expression.

II. BLACK BEAR—GUARDIAN OF THE WEST

Direction of the Home of the Waters

▲ *Introspection (self-examination)*
▲ *Healing*
▲ *Solitude*
▲ *Change*
▲ *Strength in the face of adversity*
▲ *Introversion (withdrawal from the world)*
▲ *Management of transitions*
▲ *Communication between humans and Spirit*

Color: Blue

LEGEND

In Zuni mythology, the Bear clan is believed to be in charge of the seasonal changes that bring the cold weather and snow, as well as of the diseases that frequently accompany them. As such, the bear is associated with change—it goes into hibernation in the late fall and emerges at winter's end. Though it is associated with the diseases of this seasonal period, Bear is seen not as their cause but as having the power to heal those and other illnesses.

Seasonal cycles are not Bear's only connection with change and transition. As Guardian of the West, this fetish is positioned between the South quadrant of the Medicine Wheel, which is associated with the passions of our human existence—basic drives such as fear, anger, jealousy, vengeance, avarice, greed, and so on—and the North quadrant, associated with Wisdom. All the Bear's qualities—from introspection to its ability to mediate between humans and gods—help us to transform our human passions into true wisdom.

Finally, it should be remembered that within the Zuni belief system, the most primitive and mysterious of life forms are considered to be closest to the Creator. The more fully developed the animal in terms of ego and mental development, the more difficult communication with the Creator becomes. Thus, humans, being the most "finished" of beings, are the furthest from the gods. Poshaiankia provided animals that they might aid humans in all matters of life, including communication with the gods. According to Zuni belief, Bear is our best mediator because of all the animals indigenous to the Southwest, it most nearly resembles humans.

When we meditate on Black Bear, the things that generally come to mind are tremendous power and physical strength, along with an intelligence that at times seems uncannily human yet at other times seems mysterious and almost godlike. When you hold a Bear fetish in your hand and contemplate it, you may experience its sense of inner confidence, reserve, and detachment, reminiscent of a being who is fully attuned with the natural forces.

Black Bear is invaluable whenever you are faced with change and transition in your life, whether it is a change in your livelihood, a change in a relationship with a loved one, a change in beliefs, feelings, or life perspectives, or a change in health—from health to illness and illness to health. Bear can be your ally when you are attempting to resolve conflicts, forgive yourself or others for errors of the past, or when you are faced with new challenges in your spiritual path.

It should be remembered that there is a particular kind of depression of the spirit sometimes associated with the deep introspective stage of transition and change. When this occurs, Black Bear is a reminder that there is a parallel between depression and the natural state known as hibernation—when involvement with the outer world is minimized in order to focus more energy on the inner processes necessary for a successful transition.

AFFIRMATIONS

Bear reminds us that one of the great powers we have is the power of turning to solitude and introspection, through which we integrate new experience and change. It is a power that is grossly underestimated in a society that values material productivity and external action above all else.

If you are feeling overwhelmed by events, either in the external or internal world, place Black Bear before you, its back to the west, its face to the east. Imagine it standing at the opening of a womblike cave, contemplating its spring emergence but still not ready to abandon its hibernation. It is facing the East, however, from which new light is about to emerge.

Meditate on the symbolic parallels between your present state of mind and the bear at the door of the cave. Think about the introversion (hibernating quality), the reluctance to step out of the cave, the light shining from the east.

If you are in conflict for any reason, retreat into the cave and bask for a moment in the luxury of your solitude. Remind yourself of the great strength of solitude, and be assured that no matter what the circumstances you can choose peace instead of the conflict or disturbance you are feeling.

If you feel separate and alone, remember that we are always of one spirit; the sense of separation and aloneness is simply the product of our intellect and ego. Ask Black Bear to mediate between yourself and the power that is greater than yourself, reconnecting you with the Source. Ask it for guidance in removing the self-made blocks between yourself and others and yourself and the Source.

AREAS TO EXPLORE

Our society teaches us little about how to handle transition and change effectively. Likewise, we are rarely taught how to make use of the potential power we each possess in our capacity for introspection and solitude. Use the wisdom of the Bear to help you embrace these qualities in yourself and to mark those times when circumstances in your life call upon you to make use of them.

The Bear also represents the healing power within every living organism. Explore this concept, beginning with those healing capacities such as the immune system and our bodies' ability to heal cuts and broken bones, which modern medicine recognizes; then contemplate the further healing capacities associated with the mind or spirit, such as those recognized by Native American cultures and traditional Chinese medicine.

III. BADGER—GUARDIAN OF THE SOUTH

Direction of the Place of the Beautiful Red

▲ *Aggressiveness*
▲ *Single-mindedness*
▲ *Passion*
▲ *Control*
▲ *Antidote to passivity or victimization*
▲ *Persistence in the service of a mission*
▲ *Groundedness and knowledge of the earth*

Color: Red

LEGEND

In Ashiwi mythology, Badger was assigned as Guardian of the South and the chief fetish of the Summer People. The world was seen as divided between summer and winter people. The activities of the summer people included curing and teaching; the winter people were warriors and hunters.

At first glance, Badger's aggressiveness would seem to suggest a warrior or hunter mentality. But if we study the behavior of Badger, we see that this animal is neither. Though aggressive and vicious when provoked, it does not exercise these qualities in the service of a community, as a warrior would. Moreover, since it feeds mostly on roots from the earth, it has little need to hunt.

The Badger's aggressiveness is almost entirely focused on self-defense; thus, as a healing fetish it amplifies the energy of all our natural healing processes, including those of the body. The medicine of the Badger is the single-minded, passionate defense of the organism. The person who suffers an illness frequently must overcome a sense of passivity and victimization in order to rally his or her energy for the healing process. The naturally aggressive nature of Badger lends this kind of support.

Badger symbolizes the basic, aggressive drives of human life. Driven by the ego and physical needs, the Badger can be so singularly focused on satisfying its own drives—sexuality, hunger, jealousy, acquisitiveness, fear, competitiveness, judgment of self and others, vengeance—that it would rip anything to shreds that stands in its way. This wanton destruction of others who get in our way, with no thought for such consequences as injuring the other's feelings or causing physical harm, ignores our oneness. To injure anything that is part of that oneness is to injure ourselves.

To contemplate the Badger fetish is to acknowledge that as human beings we are quite capable of being so caught up in our basic needs and so convinced that we are right that we ignore the needs of others and can become destructive. As a fetish, Badger can heal because it identifies our greatest weakness—the tendency to forget that our limited perceptions of the world are never enough and that only with our pooled spiritual resources can we even hope to come into harmony with the higher power.

AFFIRMATIONS

When you are feeling like a victim, such as during an illness or when you have given your power away to another person, hold Badger in your hand and bring to your mind the image of this animal at its most ferocious. Take in the high energy aroused by this state of being, without resorting to the destructive acts it might suggest.

Recognize that when you feel like a victim, your sense of passivity can be simply a cover for rage, which can easily become destructive. Badger is there to remind you that peace of mind and health are achieved not through mindless destruction but through a balance of action and contemplation that serves to bring harmony between the expression of our own needs and the expression of our oneness.

At times of change, when frustration runs high and fear heats us, Badger can help you either define or focus more staunchly on a goal. Change frequently involves a sense that you are fed up with the way things presently are and you want to move forward. However, running away from the present problems that are making you unhappy is the position of the victim; you lift yourself out of the victim role and begin to live more creatively and constructively when you thoughtfully establish an objective and begin to climb toward it. Badger's power, combined with his single-mindedness of purpose, can help you overcome the inertia of an unwanted way of being and launch you in the direction of your new choice.

AREAS TO EXPLORE

Badger's physique is very compact and incredibly muscular. This is a thick-skinned animal that hugs the earth almost as if a part of it. Possessing long, razor-sharp claws and razorlike teeth, Badger has the weapons to pose a threat to animals ten times its size. But its greatest defense is found in its absolute ferociousness. When this ferocity is triggered, Badger has nothing but destruction of the enemy on its mind. There is no stopping Badger from its goal of tearing the enemy to shreds.

When we humans are fearful, we are quite capable of switching into the Badger mind. Convinced that our perceptions of the world—our own thoughts, feelings, and interpretations of whatever is going on—are all that matters, we say and do things that later prove to have dire consequences. In this respect, Badger-mindedness can be the source of guilt, which is a combination of regret for having injured others and a fear of retaliation.

If we are able to acknowledge our own Badger tendencies and be aware that we have the power to choose compassion and empathy instead, a miracle occurs; our enemies become far less fearful. In the process, peaceful negotiations become possible, bringing harmony instead of war and all the grief that goes with it. The secret of managing the Badger mind is to use its energy to stop our tendency to lie around and feel helpless, vengeful, or put upon when disease or antipathy are monopolizing our attention, and then to turn that same energy into the pursuit of creative solutions.

Contemplate Badger, absolute single-mindedness, as it faces its opposite in the North, absolute knowledge. We humans always rest somewhere between these two poles, seeking the path of wisdom, which reveals that which is eternal and changeless. Though few of us will complete that path in this lifetime, having it in view as we take each small step brings a quality to our lives that we can enjoy in no other way. Be grateful to Badger for this insight.

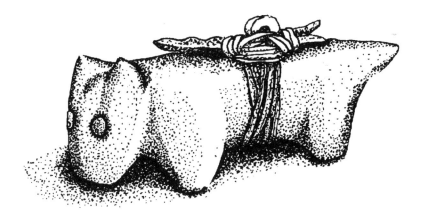

IV. WHITE WOLF—GUARDIAN OF THE EAST

Direction of the Home of the Day

▲ *Loyalty*
▲ *Insight and revelation*
▲ *Social and familial values*
▲ *Teaching and learning*
▲ *Instinct linked with intelligence*
▲ *Clarity*
▲ *Inner guidance*
▲ *Expression of personal truths*
▲ *Newness, including new choices*

Color: White

LEGEND

It is from the East that each new day comes; each reappearance of the sun provides the energy and warmth that make life possible on our planet. As Guardian of the East, White Wolf protects these phenomena—the mysteries of renewal and creation—and teaches us the truths associated with them.

Always in the position of the "new light," taken in any of its meanings—sunrise, new ideas, or truth—White Wolf also embodies the spirit of learning, of both receiving and teaching the truth. When White Wolf chooses to teach, it does so in a very particular way; always the first to see and alert us to a clear light, White Wolf does not necessarily tell us how to use that light. It is a little like the coming of each new day itself; we are given it without our asking, but we are not told how to use it, how to integrate it into our lives.

White Wolf's truths are usually communicated to us in the form of a "flash of insight" or a "glimpse" of a reality we had not previously seen. Like a bolt of lightning, such insights can change our lives, though we may have to do some hard work to integrate these new understandings with what we have known before.

If you have ever camped out under the stars and have heard the plaintive aria of a wolf filling the darkness, you will understand how this animal's truth is communicated. It would have to be described as "spine-tingling" rather than "objective," or "ecstatic" rather than "intellectual." And like any great teaching, it may be years before we are able to recognize its meaning or fully digest it.

Although wolves are mysterious creatures, they possess qualities that are remarkably human. They are highly individualistic, having personalities, physical appearances, and ways of communicating that set them apart from each other. They are highly intelligent, possessing extraordinary problem-solving skills, and they are playful. They are loving parents, with both male and female taking great pains, for many months after a litter is born, to educate their young in the ways of the world. Thus, they are excellent mediators when there are family matters to be handled.

Wolves have the capacity to express a wide range of emotion, including caring and love, steadfast loyalty, sadness, worry, grief, joy, and humor. They even laugh. However, unlike humans, wolves' expressions are always genuine, directly reflecting their inner truths rather than being "put on" for an effect.

They are social animals, forming and maintaining communities with their own kind, while maintaining strict devotion to a particular mate and their family.

AFFIRMATIONS

When confused or filled with self-doubt, hold the Wolf fetish in your hand, still your mind, and patiently wait for the truth to come. When it does, it will come either in the form of a piercing insight, like the first bright rays of a new day, or as a calm, quiet realization.

Very often, we cannot see the truth because we have filled our lives with false expectations, with deceits, or with illusions in an effort to protect ourselves from harm. Focus on the Wolf's ability to express its inner truth spontaneously, and you will be guided through the jungle of untruths, usually those of your own making, that are standing in your way.

When you have doubts about a path you are following in your life, whether it involves love relationships, livelihood, friendship, or personal development, seek the White Wolf as a guide. Imagine it standing on the path before you or watching you from a distance as you reenact, in your mind, a recent situation in which you have experienced this doubt. Allow it to observe for a time, then ask it to share its observations with you. Ask it where or why you are off course and how to get back on.

AREAS TO EXPLORE

Observe how the Wolf sits in the east, patient, confident, quiet within, as the new light breaks over the horizon and fills the sky. It greets the new light with a song, then once again becomes quiet and attentive. This is the posture of receiving the truth, of stilling the mind, of disconnecting ourselves from the half-truths and illusions that fly around inside our heads like a startled flock of starlings.

White Wolf puts itself in position to receive the truth, not by setting traps for it with reason, fear, or even hope, but through waiting with quiet patience.

With White Wolf before you or in your hand, explore how your own mind is or is not Wolflike. Ask Wolf to teach you how to sit at the edge of the world and quietly await the first light, the emergence of the truth, confident that it will come without the slightest effort on your part.

V. EAGLE—GUARDIAN OF THE UPPER REGIONS

Direction of the Home of the High

▲ *Great power and balance*
▲ *Dignity with grace*
▲ *Ability to see the "big picture"*
▲ *Grace achieved through knowledge and hard work*
▲ *Respect for the boundaries of the regions*
▲ *Connection with higher truths*
▲ *Intuitive and creative spirit*

Color: Many colors, variegated

LEGEND

To understand the power of this fetish, one needs to also have a feeling for the significance of Mother Earth, Father Sky, and Grandfather Sun. It is to the marriage between Mother Earth and Father Sky that we owe our lives, since without them we could not come into being. Nor could we live without the natural force represented by Grandfather Sun, who, with the other two, provides us with all that nourishes and sustains us.

While humans are earthbound, Eagle is most at home in the heavens, soaring effortlessly and tirelessly at great heights. As master of the heights, Eagle maintains a perfect balance between earth and sky, taking energy and light from the Sun. With the symbolic references of Sky being to our spiritual nature, Earth to our physical nature, and Sun to our life energies, Eagle offers guidance for bringing about balance and harmony among these three essential forces.

In Ashiwi mythology, there is a story about a boy with a pet eagle who becomes so enamored of the bird that he flies away with it, forsaking his bonds with his human family and community. He falls in love with a beautiful Eagle maiden and marries her.

Among the Eagle people he runs up against some real problems. He cannot eat the uncooked flesh that is their mainstay. So his wife takes him to the west where the Stork people feed him beans, a diet closer to his own. The Stork people receive him openly but warn him never to go to the land in the South, which is the region of Death.

His Eagle wife warns him likewise. She tells him that he must make a choice between her love for him and his own curiosity about Death. The boy fails to heed either the Stork people or his wife. He indulges his curiosity about Death and goes to its village, finally taking part in its ceremonies and lying with several beautiful maidens there.

Upon awakening the next morning, the boy is surrounded by death and decay. When Death pursues him, he escapes only with the help of the Badger people. But although he escapes, neither his wife and her people nor the Stork people will take him back. He has been unfaithful to them all, has failed to honor their knowledge, and has placed the indulgence of his own desires above their love. So, too, has he dishonored the people of his human home.

He implores his wife and her people to receive him, but they refuse. They tell him that he cannot survive with them or anywhere else without love and honor, and he has proved himself incapable of both. However, the elders finally convince his wife to return him to his own people on Mother Earth. This she does, depositing him in the middle of his village, where he instantly perishes.

The story teaches about love, honor for one's people, and a recognition that we must accept our human identity and limitations. The boy's effort to escape from these truths leads him to an unbalanced life with his Eagle wife and the Stork people. Finally, in his arrogance, he seeks to know Death, thus committing the final violation in assuming that he can mingle with the gods. His selfish and arrogant path leads him so far afield that he has no clear identity, and finally he must perish.

In all this, the Eagle represents the wisdom to see but at the same time to honor the boundaries between Earth, Sky, and the Gods. The final lesson is that we can borrow the Eagle's sight—its ability to survey all six regions—but we need first to learn to honor and love our human identity and the boundaries between the six regions.

AFFIRMATIONS

If you feel muddled or uncertain about any issue, seek the vision of the Eagle to guide you. Imagine yourself soaring above your troubles like this great bird, able to survey all that lies below you with great accuracy. Temporarily detached from everyday life in this way, you can begin to look more closely at the issues and people who are troubling you. With the knowledge gained in this way, return to Earth, reminding yourself that while useful in the short run, the vision of the Eagle can only be borrowed. To honor your humanness—through your loyalty and love for all that the Earth provides—is your first duty.

When you feel that your life is out of balance, you can seek Eagle's guidance, asking for help in determining what qualities you need to strengthen in each of the six regions. Being able to see the "big picture," Eagle may refer you to any or all of the other Guardians, suggesting that you hold a dialogue with those who can provide the specific guidance and support you need.

AREAS TO EXPLORE

Bring to your mind the image of the great soaring Eagle, the most majestic and powerful of all birds. Focus on the fact that its flight, so strong and grand, is made possible by something that is invisible—the air. Air is much like thought and like that invisible world the native peoples called "spirit." Yet this is the Eagle's home and the medium in which it is most powerful. Explore how these forces work in your own life—how the invisible world of thoughts, feelings, and spirit sustains you, carries you forward, allows you to soar like the Eagle. Explore also how these invisible forces hinder you—how dark thoughts buffet your flight, driving you earthward; how you feel when the spirit of love temporarily vanishes. Give gratitude to the invisible world, recognizing that your mind and spirit, like the Eagle, are sustained and nurtured by it.

VI. MOLE—GUARDIAN OF THE LOWER REGIONS

Direction of the Home of the Low

▲ *Connection with the energies of the earth*
▲ *Knowledge of herbs, roots, minerals, seeds, rivers,
and other hidden bounties of the earth*
▲ *Sensitivity to touch and vibration, the kinesthetic sense*
▲ *Ability to turn inward*
▲ *Introspection and blindness to all but light and dark in the material world*
▲ *Love expressed in nature*
▲ *Awareness of subtle energies and influences*

Color: Black

LEGEND

Numerous Zuni stories tell how Mole helped in the hunt. When the hunters had spotted their prey, they would ask the prey fetishes for assistance. In the hunters' prayers, they treated Mole as possessing powers to control the trees and underbrush. They would ask the branches and underbrush of the forest to reach out and slow down the animal being pursued. Similarly, they would ask Mole to soften the earth so that the prey would not be able to leap or run fast.

In the Zuni tales, Mole is usually credited with having a certain cunning and an ironical sense of humor. For example, in a story reminiscent of the classic "Race of the Hare and Tortoise," Mole challenges all comers in the annual *tikwa*, or "kicked-stick" race, in which neighboring tribes competed with each other. Mole wins the race by communicating with its cousins under the earth. At each checkpoint on the race, Mole pops up its head, showing the other runners that it is far ahead of them. Of course, what the runners don't realize is that the Mole that makes its announcement each time isn't the same one that started the race with them. The whole thing has been planned far ahead by the Mole people's entire underground city, with Mole's friends and relatives, alerted by the sound of the native runners overhead, popping up at each checkpoint.

Thereafter, whenever the kicked-stick race was run, native runners sought the help of the Mole people, asking them to make the ground infirm for the competition and to dig caverns so that their opponents' sticks would be swallowed up by the earth.

Though the smallest and least powerful in terms of its physical prowess, Mole is nevertheless an important fetish. First and foremost, its smallness helps us to focus on those small changes that ultimately make a great difference in our lives. To understand this power, consider the role that small details play in our lives. One of the best examples of this that I have ever heard came from a client of mine who is an airline pilot.

One day when we were discussing the power and importance of small changes in our lives, this pilot's eyes lit up, and he said that he finally got it. "It's like flying an airplane," he said. "If you are making a cross-country flight, the tiniest error in the compass can throw you off course by thousands of miles. It is the same in our lives. The tiniest change made each day may not seem like much at the time, but if you hold that course of tiny increments you're going to come out in a year, or five, or at the end of your life, in a very different place than you otherwise would. And because each tiny increment of change is so small, we'll experience very little resistance along the way."

A similar observation about the power of smallness is expressed in the aphorism "If everyone were to light just one candle, what a bright world this would be." There are also parables in the Eastern philosophies that speak of the tiny trickle of water that over time creates huge chasms and ultimately great rivers. We are here reminded that our own small actions, especially choices we make for the common good, are tremendously important, though it is often difficult to imagine that one person can really make a difference.

In healing, Mole is able to reach into the deepest and smallest of the mysteries for us, touching and bringing back to us knowledge so subtle as to elude our everyday attention. Its knowledge of herbs and of the roots and undersides of plants puts it in touch with a chemistry that still eludes modern chemists and physicians. Mole reminds us of the shamans who speak of the "healing spirits" of the plants and rituals that they employ to effect change.

Mole provides awareness and knowledge of the subtle, rather than the gross, powers—such powers as intuitive insight, an understanding of the vegetable world, and the use of subtle energies in such healing practices as acupuncture and homeopathy.

AFFIRMATIONS

Whenever you feel discouraged by an objective or mission that seems unobtainable, seek the help of Mole to guide you in the best use of the power of the small. Be reminded that you have great power at your disposal when you persistently make tiny increments of change.

In any healing quest, whether it lies in the physical, emotional, or spiritual realm, seek Mole's knowledge about the subtle influences in our lives. In physical healing, Mole might help you focus your powers to stimulate the immune system; it might help you access your natural powers for mending flesh and bone or even help influence the microorganisms or out-of-control cells that are factors in many diseases. With emotional matters, Mole can advise with those thoughts, feelings, and perceptions that cast shadows on ourselves and our relationships. For example, when the darkness of self-doubt stops us from pursuing a goal we value highly, we can ask for Mole's help to remove it. In spiritual matters, Mole is particularly helpful in revealing our subtle relationships with the vegetable world—the forests, herbs, and very chemistry of the soil that help to keep the earth in balance.

AREAS TO EXPLORE

One of the important teachings in native cultures is that only when we are standing firmly on our own soil can we hope to live in harmony with nature and the gods. With Mole, explore those choices you have made in your life that presently undermine you, that soften the soil under your feet, tripping you up or making your passage in the world unsteady. Make your footing more solid by seeking Mole's knowledge of the most basic sources of your support—other people, your feelings about yourself, and your sense of your own physical "center." For example, sedentary people or those who live primarily in their heads sometimes lose all sense of their physical nature. Losing this physical center can result in accidental bodily injuries and an inability to enjoy the senses; exercise as simple as daily walks or as complex as taking a class in the martial arts can restore this balance.

Finally, experiment with this fetish in a natural setting, asking it to help you communicate with the subtle spiritual energies of plants and other creatures of the Mole world.

VII. COYOTE

▲ *Self-centeredness*

▲ *Crazy wisdom*

▲ *Buffoonery*

▲ *Arrogance*

▲ *Personification of the "human comedy"*

▲ *Vanity*

▲ *The "trickster"*

▲ *Clownishness*

▲ *Ability to laugh at one's own mistakes*

▲ *The antihero whose antics make it easier to see ourselves*

▲ *Puppet of the gods*

LEGEND

In most Native American cultures, Coyote is depicted as the "trickster," a kind of practical joker who is always clowning around and causing mostly minor problems. But a reading of a cross-section of the tales from various tribes reveals that Coyote is also quite a complex character, indeed.

Coyote embodies the single characteristic that makes human life most difficult: vanity, or an inflated sense of self-importance. As often as not, the tales describe a male coyote. Don Quixote Coyote, for instance, is so wrapped up in himself that he is totally convinced that his interpretations of events in the world and his opinions of other creatures are correct beyond question. He never doubts that his own perceptions reflect how the world really is. Similarly, he is so focused on satisfying his own selfish needs that he will do almost anything—lie, cheat, con, or steal—to get his way. These same qualities make him easy prey for anyone who wants to manipulate him—and others often do, motivated by little more than the amusement that comes from outwitting him.

Most Coyote stories are extended jokes, and in these the humor is nearly always at Coyote's own expense. However, the stories are generally told to point out our own human weaknesses so that we can learn to laugh at them. As often as not, there are morals to the Coyote stories, warning us against certain kinds of behavior, particularly those associated with selfishness and arrogance.

Coyote is usually depicted as being at least two steps ahead of himself, so eager that he is constantly tripping over his own feet, actually and figuratively. In his eagerness to catch some animal he is pursuing, he will often act impulsively, giving himself away and causing his prey to take flight long before he is ready to capture it.

In spite of his shortcomings—his arrogance, selfishness, clumsiness, and all the rest—he can be a great teacher. When the Ashiwi use this fetish for help in the hunt, Coyote generally takes on a more noble demeanor. He seems to have great wisdom to pass onto others, but he cannot make use of it himself, owing to his impetuous nature.

Coyote is more antihero than hero. Seeing the consequences of his inability to give much thought to others' needs and perceptions, we are better able to recognize the limits of our own selfishness and thus correct our ways, becoming more compassionate and caring. Seeing the consequences of his lack of courage, we are better able to acknowledge the need for that quality in ourselves. Seeing the consequences of his impetuousness, clumsiness, and greed, we are better able to understand the value of transcending the same qualities in ourselves.

Almost wholly focused on satisfying his bodily needs and his ego, along with his infamous need to play tricks on other people, Coyote might be seen as a villain. But in fact he is often an endearing figure, only because he is also a buffoon. His tricks and devious plans nearly always backfire on him, making him take the brunt of his own jokes. Nobody else suffers, and Coyote himself appears to be quite indestructible.

Many times in the traditional legends, Coyote is used by the gods to reveal certain lessons to humanity. They use him not to punish us but to lead us closer to self-knowledge and wisdom by making us the target of Coyote's tricks. We learn not so much through the pain or embarrassment of being his victim but through narrowly escaping this fate. We receive the lesson afterward, when we understand how closely we courted disaster by indulging the vanities of selfishness, greed, and arrogance.

AFFIRMATIONS

When life is becoming confusing and stressful, place Coyote before you and play with the possibility that what you are experiencing might be one of Coyote's tricks. Is it possible that by stepping back just a little bit you may be able to catch a glimpse of Coyote and then outwit the Trickster at his own game?

When you are confronted with people who take themselves too seriously, who are being arrogant and selfish, rest assured that they are manifesting the Coyote nature that lives in all of us. If you simply stand out of their way and stay with your own truth, they will eventually, like Coyote, trip themselves up. Never go into combat with such people. Your best defense is to stick to paths that do not cross theirs.

AREAS TO EXPLORE

There's more than a little Coyote in all of us. He represents our willingness to believe that the etheric world we create in our minds is more important than the world *out there*. He is our tendency to want to prove to the rest of the world that our perceptions and interpretations, our feelings and our needs are more urgent, more important, more useful, or more accurate than anyone else's. Coyote is blind to higher truths than his own.

Holding Coyote in our hands or placing him before us in plain sight, we can contemplate all the ways in which he mirrors us. One of the greatest and most difficult lessons Coyote provides is that what we consider our greatest strengths may at the same time be our greatest weaknesses. For example, the industriousness and tenacity that make us successful in a career or business venture may be the very qualities that make it difficult for us to enjoy more intimate relationships. To be relaxed and enjoy playfulness or "aimless activities" with our friends goes against the grain of our tenacious or industrious nature. Similarly, our skill for helping other people in crisis may make us easy prey to the manipulations of those with less noble intentions.

Contemplate Coyote and implant this Trickster in your mind as a reminder of the human condition. By personifying our vanities, he allows us to study ourselves more easily, to clarify what it is we do to make our lives difficult. In the face of this antihero's buffoonery, we can laugh at ourselves and choose to follow other paths that promise greater peace, happiness, and prosperity.

VIII. SNAKE—WILOLOANE

▲ *Exploration of the mysteries of life*
▲ *Elemental or primitive energy*
▲ *Zigzagging and slithering motion*
▲ *Elusiveness*
▲ *Personification of lightning*

LEGEND

In the Ashiwi cosmology, all the various life forms are classified according to their closeness to the Creator, with the most primitive and elemental forms being closest and the more complex forms being furthest away. Thus, human beings, who are considered to be the most "finished" and most complicated, are the furthest away, while Snake is simplest and thus closest to the invisible reality that we associate with spirit.

For the European mind, this is not an easy concept to grasp. We like to think of ourselves as the most spiritual, the closest to God, and the highest of life forms. The Ashiwis' seeming contradiction of this idea can best be understood by thinking in terms of instincts versus intellect. The snake, being one of the least "finished" of beings, has little or no free will and is capable of only the most rudimentary choices. Its life is ruled by its instincts, and these are dictated at birth by an inner program given to the snake by the Creator. In this way, the snake is most dependent on the Creator and other outside influences; it reacts to the world rather than making independent choices.

The Ashiwi cosmology contains a hierarchy at the top of which are the elements of nature, such as lightning, rain, and the light of the sun, because they are not mortal but everlasting. By this measure, we humans are the least powerful because we have extremely short lives compared to the elements.

Also in the Ashiwi cosmology, plants, animals, and inanimate objects that have qualities similar to the elements of nature are believed to be most directly related to them. Thus, Snake is seen as a personification of lightning because its shape and movements resemble a bolt of lightning flashing across the sky. Indeed, the Snake's ancient name, *Wiloloane*, is derived from the Zuni word for the serpentine movements of both lightning and snakes.

Human beings, by contrast, resemble very little in nature except themselves. But this is not all that distances them from the Creator. We also have complex brains that allow us to reason things out, to make choices and decisions that are relatively independent of the Creator. While this makes us more "finished" than other earth creatures, our complex brains are also the source of our feelings of longing for connection, our feelings that we are abandoned and alone. It is because of our own complex nature that we seek various rituals to reclaim our contact with the eternal forces and the mysteries that bind us to the universe.

In most of the Zuni stories, if a human being wants to communicate with the Creator or with other gods or forces in the world, he or she must find an animal who will serve as mediator. And in order for the communication to be complete, the person must choose the animal that is most nearly like himself or herself. Thus, you might choose as your mediator Bear, who of all the animals of the part of the world known by the Ashiwi most nearly resembles the human being.

All of this is by way of explaining how we might use Snake as a fetish. Although Snake least resembles us, it is like us in a single respect: we are both mortal. Snake is more closely aligned with nature and the eternal, however, because it personifies lightning, one of the most elemental forces in nature. Snake, then, is perhaps our closest connection with the immortal power of lightning; thus, it serves as a kind of amplifier. When a drawing, painting, or a carved bit of shell in the shape of a snake or lightning bolt is attached to a fetish, it increases the power of that fetish.

A Snake fetish alone provides us with a reminder of the eternal powers of nature, powers we share only insofar as we embody the life force itself. Though our physical bodies are mortal, the life force that animates them is eternal. This eternal force is the source of any transformational powers that we are capable of possessing and experiencing. These powers include a willingness to be receptive to life, an openness to change, the power to heal, and the ability to intuit our connection with powers greater than ourselves.

AFFIRMATIONS

When your energy is low, as during periods following great stress, during a period of great change, or during an illness, bring Snake's presence into any work you might do with the fetishes. For example, combining the powers of Snake and Badger can amplify the sense of groundedness that Badger can provide. Similarly, Snake can amplify Badger's power to keep you single-minded in your pursuit of a path out of your present dilemma. Any qualities that your other fetishes possess for you will be amplified by Snake's presence.

When you are feeling that life is out of control, use the Snake fetish to remind you of your essential connection with the immortal. No matter how alone you are feeling, no matter how much you may feel that only your own efforts matter, Snake can remind you that we are all interconnected in ways that transcend what we know of time and space. We can call upon the higher powers that are in charge of all this (the Ashiwi called them "Keepers of the Way") anytime we wish. Through recognizing this eternal interrelationship, we can begin to recognize that we are never alone and that our belief that only our own efforts can save us is an illusion, an invention of our Coyote nature.

AREAS TO EXPLORE

Snake is a reminder of our connection with the eternal forces of nature. However, if you have grown up in the Judeo-Christian tradition, which associates the Snake with original sin, you may initially feel a great repulsion for this fetish. This repulsion can make it difficult to see Snake in Ashiwi terms, as our means of connection with the mysteries of the invisible reality and the life force itself.

If you have difficulty relating to Snake as a fetish, try looking on it as the personification of those vast energies we see expressed in lightning, that most powerful of the natural forces. Through this perception of Snake, you can let yourself be open to the awesome powers that are immortal and eternal rather that mortal and temporal. These elemental forces are all essential to the ongoing Creation in which we all take part.

IX. RAVEN

▲ *Magic and sorcery*
▲ *Transformational powers*
▲ *Guidance for deeper understanding of the shadow self*
▲ *Courage and comfort with the darkness*

LEGEND

Although Raven is not one of the original Zuni fetishes, this bird does appear again and again in Ashiwi stories. In recent years a few Zuni fetish carvers have begun producing small figures of these birds. They are generally not carved in the crude, rudimentary style typical of the original fetishes but are more realistic, rather like small sculptures.

Whether traditional fetishes or not, these Raven figures can be useful to anyone responsive to them. In Zuni legends, this bird is often associated with a special type of magical playfulness. While it can seem that the Raven is playing tricks similar to those that Coyote plays, Raven is far more adept, far more clever than Coyote, and not focused on selfish intent. Raven's magic plays an important role in the medicine of transformation, while Coyote's tricks teach us about our limits and foibles as mortals.

In one traditional Zuni story, two Ravens are sitting on a stone spire in the mountains, "racing their eyes." They point out a distant spot on the desert, marked by a rock or a tree. Then their eyes pop out of their heads and race to the landmark like arrows shot from a great bow. Afterward, their eyes return, slipping easily back into their sockets. The two Ravens are just delighted with this game, which is a tribute to their magical powers.

Coyote, who is strolling by, watches the Ravens and begs them to show him how to race his own eyes. They try to warn him against this, pointing out that he cannot command the magic they possess. When, however, he makes a pest of himself by insisting that they teach him, they tell him to lie down and get prepared for a little pain. This said, they pluck out his eyes, swallow them, and disappear into the distance.

Coyote lies out in the sun for the rest of the day, waiting for his eyes to return. Finally, he sets off, feeling his way, still unable to understand where he went wrong. Eventually he replaces his eyes with cranberries—ones that have not yet ripened and are still yellow. This is how Coyote came to have yellow eyes while all other animals have black ones. It also accounts for why Coyote's sight is not very good and why he is such a poor hunter.

The Ravens thus teach Coyote a hard-won lesson, that their special magic is not to be taken lightly and is certainly not to be used by the likes of him. On a deeper level, this suggests that Raven's magic, to be employed in healing, does not belong to gross physical reality. Rather, we should be very clear about confining its use to the non-physical plane.

We may call upon Raven to work with us through our dreams, remembering that it is on this nonmaterial level that all creative change begins. No significant human action is possible without the prior formation of that action in our minds, as idea, dream, or visualization.

In the inner world where Raven is most at home, we encounter our own shadow self. This is the part of ourselves that we would just as soon keep buried. The shadow self is the dark side of our everyday self, which because it has experienced early pain or rejection prefers to hide out. The challenge comes when we discover that it is a tremendous drain on our energy to keep this aspect of ourselves hidden. In fact, once we get to know the shadow self, it can become an invaluable source of wisdom, compassion, and insight.

Our fear of the shadow self is natural. However, to keep this aspect of ourselves buried is to neglect one of our greatest personal resources. Our personal power depends on our ability to come face to face with the fears that the shadow self harbors, a process that ultimately frees us of those same fears in the external world. Raven is a great ally for our going deeply into this shadow reality, since Raven has no fear of this inner territory.

AFFIRMATIONS

At dark moments, when confronted with personal failure, limitations, loss, or self-knowledge that is troubling, seek the assistance of Raven. Imagine Raven flying deep into the darkness of your interior world, where dreams and distressing thoughts and feelings are first seeded. Notice that Raven is comfortable, for it knows that anything we have the courage to see can be transformed. Raven offers courage and support in this territory and with those aspects of yourself that you would rather deny. Ask for Raven's help, making specific requests for help with making peace with your shadow self.

With any introspective process, call upon Raven to be your guide. In that world, ask Raven to perform any magic, any miracles you desire, as long as they are ultimately for the common good. If your request is a noble one, you will be rewarded; if it is selfish, as it was for Coyote when he lost his eyes, you will first experience Raven's resistance. If Raven says no or tells you that you are off base in your request, respect this response. Do not press for something that will not be helpful to you.

AREAS TO EXPLORE

Imagine that the inner world of your consciousness is a vast space, filled with mystery. Our usual window into this world is the dream. However, with the aid of Raven, you can freely and safely explore this world while you are awake. With Raven as your companion, you can come face to face with your shadow self or other aspects of your life that you would not otherwise be comfortable exploring. Raven directs you, guides you, supports you, assuring you that there is no harm in knowing; there is only harm in not knowing.

When you are seeking change in a relationship, in your career, or in any other aspect of life, request Raven's assistance. The transformational magic that Raven can work for you, although it occurs only in the invisible inner world, is the first step toward finding your true path in any quest, whether it is a spiritual, relational, career-centered, or economic one. Listen for Raven's stories, related to you through your mind's eye—in dreams, imaginary conversations, images, and hunches. With your careful consideration of the consequences—positive and negative—and with your active participation in bringing them to fruition in the physical world, your dreams will eventually come true.

X. FALCON—YOUNGER BROTHER OF THE EAGLE

▲ *Power and harmony*
▲ *Ability to see the "big picture"*
▲ *Grace achieved through knowledge and hard work*
▲ *Telepathic communication with other people or animals*
▲ *Intuitive and creative spirit*

LEGEND

In the original cosmology, in which Poshaiankia names the animals, Falcon is called the "younger brother of the Eagle." This bird is credited with having many of the same qualities as Eagle, only to a lesser degree. For this reason, the reader should refer back to the Eagle reading for more information on this fetish.

The Zuni stories make a few important distinctions between Falcon and Eagle. The first is the difference in size and power. The eagle that the Zunis usually refer to is the bald eagle, which is approximately three to four times as large as most falcons. Thus, we must assume that Falcon is considerably less powerful and considerably less important as a fetish than an Eagle fetish would be. Another important distinction has to do with the hunting habits of the two birds of prey. In one traditional story, the people call upon Falcon rather than Eagle for help because the former hunts closer to the ground and thus is better able to see small creatures hiding behind rocks or in the bushes. In this case, the people felt that Eagle's loftiness would be a handicap.

The stories of Falcon give the impression that this bird was much more approachable than the greater Eagle. In a number of Zuni and other Native American stories, the Falcon is seen as a personal messenger, carrying information to other people or between people and animals. The Eagle is seen as much more powerful medicine, reserved for only the highest missions between people and the higher powers, such as Grandfather Sky, thunder and lightning, or other gods associated with the sky or the mountains.

AFFIRMATIONS

If you feel unclear or you lack confidence, call upon Falcon for guidance and advice. Imagine that Falcon is soaring above you, looking out over all that concerns you at this time, but with a sharp eye for details that you cannot see. Falcon provides you with a bigger picture than you are able to see from the ground yet still keeps the attention focused on practicalities, in contrast to the more abstract, philosophical, and universal focus of Eagle. See for a moment with the eyes of Falcon, not from the lofty pinions of Eagle but from a slightly more mundane and "earthly" vantage point.

If you wish to communicate with people far away, imagine Falcon carrying your message to them. Look upon Falcon as your personal message bearer. Visualize Falcon winging its way to your friend, then circling that person until he or she looks up. At the moment your friend looks up, your message will arrive, as if telepathically.

AREAS TO EXPLORE

Look again at the reading for Eagle, as much of it applies to Falcon.

In addition, experiment with Falcon in the development of your intuitive abilities. For example, visualize the Falcon as being capable of flying deep into your own consciousness, and through your consciousness, linking up with the infinite consciousness of the entire world—what the Hopis call the "web that connects us all." Free to fly wherever it wishes in this region, this bird is a constant messenger between you and people who are emotionally or spiritually close to you.

As Falcon becomes an increasingly familiar figure in your mind's eye, pay attention when it appears. Stop and listen. See if Falcon has a message for you, then follow through. If your Falcon tells you that a friend is seeking you, call that friend or write to him or her. Make contact. If you wish to alert a friend or share a piece of information, you might do so by sending a message through Falcon or by having Falcon tell your friend to contact you. And, of course, when it seems urgent, contact your friend in person; especially during crises we tend to lose trust in, or simply forget, our intuitive assets.

There are also stories of people who use this bird to communicate with their domestic animals, such as a cat, dog, or horse they are training, or with a sick animal who needs their help.

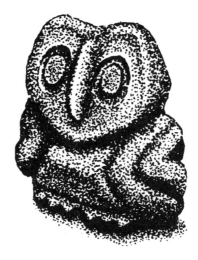

OWL—NIGHT BIRD

▲ *The medicine of sorcery*
▲ *Magical transformation*
▲ *Link between the dark, unseen world and the world of light*
▲ *Communication between spiritual and physical realities*
▲ *Comfort with the shadow self*

LEGEND

It is rare to find genuine Zuni fetishes of Owls. However, small realistic figures of the owl, carved by modern Zuni craftspeople, are now quite popular and readily available.

It seems odd that this bird was not more frequently used as a fetish since the animal itself plays a prominent role in many ancient Zuni stories, where it is depicted as having magical powers. Its magic derives from the fact that the nocturnal Owl lives comfortably with the darkness. It is not only capable of seeing in the dark but it also flies and hunts at night. In early times, native peoples must have found this to be a source of great wonder, since they knew that they themselves had only limited night vision.

Throughout human history and on every continent, darkness has been associated with the unknown; it is the place of mystery and sometimes evil. While the Zunis did not see Owls as evil, they certainly did see them as mysterious.

Owl's ability to cross back and forth between the seen and unseen worlds won it the reputation for possessing transformational powers, capable of changing itself from one form to another—from Owl to human and from human back to Owl. In one Zuni story,[1] transcribed by Frank Hamilton Cushing in the late 1890s, Owl plays an important part in the tale of two young lovers.

The story goes that during the lovers' courting, the young man is tricked by his lover's jealous sister into accidentally killing the beautiful young woman whom he longed to marry. After her death, the young man is inconsolable. Wanting to comfort him, the spirit of the dead lover leaves her grave and comes to him. She tells him that since she is a spirit and he a mere mortal, they can never be together as husband and wife. But he is so much in love with her that he continues to pursue her on her journey to the Land of the Spirits, which one enters through a beautiful lake, called the Lake of the Dead.

Being a spirit, the young woman, of course, has no difficulty entering the Land of the Spirits, but the young man, being mortal, cannot follow. Soon Owl appears and takes him to his own home in the mountains. There Owl is transformed into a man who introduces the young man to his family. The young man tells his woeful story, and the Owl agrees to help him, offering him a magical medicine that will allow him to sleep.

Owl tells the young man that he will sleep deeply and then will awaken and find his young lover beside him. At this point, Owl warns, she will still be a spirit, and he must not touch her. But if he journeys with her back to the land of his fathers and does not touch her along the way, all will be well and she will be changed back into her physical form.

In the beginning, all goes as the Owl promised. But as the two young lovers journey back, the young woman stops to rest. While she sleeps, the young man gazes upon her and is so touched by her beauty and his love for her that he leans over and kisses her. In that instant, just as the Owl had warned, the lovers are separated forever, she as a spirit, he as a mortal.

This story is part of the Ashiwi cosmology that explains how the spiritual and physical worlds came to be separated by death. Although the Ashiwis acknowledge that this separation causes much sadness for those who live on, still they feel that this plan for the world is a good one. Without separation between the spiritual and the physical, the storyteller reflects, the world would be overrun with people, causing starvation and wars.

In this, as in other legends, Owl acts as a mediator between the spiritual and physical worlds. At home in either, Owl has much wisdom concerning the world of spirit and can communicate some of this knowledge to us through sleep.

AFFIRMATIONS

When separated from those you love and longing to be close to them, let Owl be your guide, reuniting you through recalling important moments you shared with these people. Hold Owl's image in your mind, then imagine it slowly transforming into the image of your missing friend.

When puzzled, confused, or in conflict, call upon the Owl fetish to fly deep into the darkest recesses of your consciousness. Here it will encounter your shadow self, consisting of those aspects of yourself that you would rather hide. Owl will remind you that you cannot be free of such influences until you stop denying and resisting them and allow them to come forth into awareness. Through Owl's help, you can face what you fear and be free of it forever. Then puzzlement, confusion, and conflict will give way to new clarity and peace.

AREAS TO EXPLORE

Most of us fear the unknown, especially the unknown in ourselves. Owl reminds us that true wisdom comes from having the courage to transform the unknown in ourselves into the known. In moments of quiet introspection, call upon Owl to support you, helping you to find the courage you need in order to fly in the darkness, that is, travel beyond fear. With its perfect nocturnal vision, let Owl fly into those unknown regions within you, bringing back into the light the source of the fears that you are now ready to face.

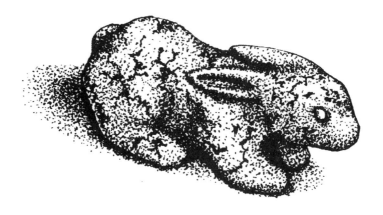

XII. RABBIT

▲ *Playful "trickster"*
▲ *Crazy wisdom*
▲ *Irony aimed at getting us to look at ourselves*
▲ *Representative of the world of illusion and double meanings*
▲ *Guile*
▲ *Paradox and contradiction*
▲ *Example of living by one's wits*

LEGEND

While the rabbit is not generally looked upon as an actual fetish, in recent times it has become a popular subject for fetish carvers. Zuni carvers have made figures of these animals available partly because of their general popularity but also because they are often called upon to make fetishes for other Native Americans, including various tribes throughout the Midwest and Great Lakes area. For some people of these areas, Rabbit has played a role similar to the one played by Coyote in the Southwest and West—that of the trickster.

Rabbit is different from Coyote in that we are at first taken in by its gentleness, subtlety, and charm, all of which can seem to contradict its trickster nature; Coyote, of course, has none of these qualities and is usually depicted as the epitome of coarse and antisocial behavior. While the jokes, trickery, and manipulativeness of Rabbit might be compared to Coyote's, the former's are generally gentle and ultimately compassionate rather than selfish or mean-spirited, as Coyote's are. Rabbit's trickery often is intended to reveal a lesson for the common good, rather than being totally motivated by vanity.

Instead of being vain and arrogant like Coyote, Rabbit has a strong awareness of others, though, of course, this animal is no great altruist, either. Rabbit's gentle virtues come from the obvious fact that it is among the smaller animals, has neither speed nor great strength, neither claws nor teeth that can tear, like Coyote. While Coyote is carnivorous, Rabbit is a vegetarian and knows little of killing. Rabbit depends for its survival on its sensitive hearing, its quick reflexes, its wit, and its ability to smell danger long before it arrives. Much of Rabbit's trickery grows out of its need to protect itself. After all, many animals, such as wildcats, coyotes, wolves, mountain lions, eagles, falcons, and humans, seek out Rabbit for its flesh. To outwit those who would have Rabbit for dinner, it must keep its senses as sharp as its wits.

Out of fear, Rabbit is frequently overeager. Always on the lookout for those who would make it their dinner, Rabbit is prone to acting impulsively, giving itself away, and thus turning its worst fears into self-fulfilling prophecies. Though Rabbit resorts to its wits to save itself, it is not always successful in doing so. Rabbit never seems to learn that instead of trying to trick or manipulate others, it can be successful in life only by staying focused on itself.

At least one ancient tale speculates that Rabbit's most important survival method may in fact be its prolific reproductive capacities. And thus the most valuable lesson Rabbit may have to pass along to us is that only the spirit that animates our physical bodies is immortal while the physical form itself is transitory.

Like Coyote's, Rabbit's antics allow us to see our own limits and to correct our errors, thus becoming more forgiving, compassionate, and caring of ourselves and others. All these are qualities that the great spiritual teachers of every continent tell us that we must develop both for our own peace of mind and for our survival as a race. Seeing the consequences of Rabbit's timidity, for example, we are better able to see the necessity for calling upon our own inner strength. Seeing Rabbit's tendency to project its worst fears into realities that justify those fears, sometimes causing its own destruction, we recognize the need to look inward and master our own fears.

AFFIRMATIONS

When you are feeling confused about a relationship or about a decision you have made, place Rabbit before you and ask if this confusion in merely one of its tricks. Is there a double meaning that you are missing? A contradiction? Is there a lesson you are supposed to learn, one that you can only get by looking past what appear to be your only choices and seeing others that are less obvious?

When you are challenged by stubbornness, or by authority figures who are arbitrary or inflexible, bring Rabbit out and question it. You can be certain that Rabbit has put this person on your path to get you to reflect on your own stubbornness and inflexibility. Though you may have a little or a lot, try letting go of these qualities in yourself and see if the other person doesn't let up and begin listening to you. Seek a means of staying with your own truth without projecting a defensive stand that will arouse a combative posture in others.

AREAS TO EXPLORE

The Rabbit trickster is in all of us. Rabbit is the magician in our minds, who creates what isn't there—the fear that is not justified by the actual events, the wishful thinking, and even such mundane mind tricks as convincing yourself you can afford to buy something when you cannot.

Use Rabbit to help you explore the various ways that your own creative powers work both for and against you. For example, it is your creative ability that sets up fears about things that haven't happened and maybe never will happen. It is this same creative ability that, mixed with fear, can tell you not to trust the "intuition" or "hunch" that you just know is right.

Seek to understand the double meanings that Rabbit is capable of creating through irony, paradox, and contradiction. Note that these appear in our lives only under very specific circumstances—mainly when we project only two possible alternatives or answers to a problem or question. Irony, paradox, and contradiction all fade when we seek a third solution, thus acknowledging that there are probably an infinite number of solutions to virtually every situation. We open our eyes to these other solutions only when we begin entertaining the possibility that it is only the Rabbit tricks of our minds that make it appear there are only two.

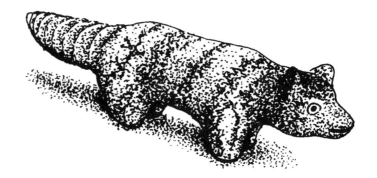

XIII. FOX

▲ *Cleverness*
▲ *Observational skills*
▲ *Loyalty and protectiveness of family and friends*
▲ *Ability to disappear into the landscape*
▲ *Clarity about the value of blending in*

LEGEND

Experienced hunters, who depend upon wild game as food, know Fox as one of the most elusive of animals. Since it has very little meat on its thin, wiry body, it is not an animal that one would pursue for dinner. Instead, it is a presence in the forest, competing with the hunter for small game such as rabbits or game birds.

This beautiful animal is almost ghostlike in the forest, appearing and disappearing like a hallucination. Quick on its feet, it shifts around on the forest floor, weaving mysteriously through the shadows and foliage.

A fox will track a hunter, observing him or her from a great distance. If that hunter gets too close to the den where Fox's family is hidden, it will cause a distraction, making itself known so that the hunter will be led away from the Fox's home.

For the hunter, the experience of being observed by a fox is an eerie one. The animal is so clever, making itself visible or invisible at will, that the hunter may feel his or her mind is simply playing tricks. It sometimes seems that this is the Fox's purpose, to play with the hunter's own self-doubts.

The energy of the Fox is like that of no other animal. One is acutely aware of its keen mind and its cleverness. It seems to approach life with an attitude of amusement, almost condescension, at least where we humans are concerned. It observes the antics of humans with mild interest, as if it cannot quite imagine why one would approach life in such an unnecessarily complicated way.

Like Wolf, Fox is family-oriented, protecting, nurturing, and educating its kits until they are able to make their own way safely in the world. Fox families are closely bonded, keeping in constant touch through a few short, sharp barks even when they hunt for game far from home.

AFFIRMATIONS

Whenever you feel threatened, either emotionally or physically, take a lesson from Fox, blending in with the landscape so that you almost become a part of it. In a crowd, blend into the spaces between others, mimicking their postures and movements so that your own become indistinguishable from theirs.

In conflicts where there is no chance of being heard or where there is nothing to be gained by trying, disappear into silence. Offer only the illusion of agreement and then seek a safe escape route.

When you want to gather information and observe with a sense of detachment, seek the aid of Fox. Even if the person or event you wish to study and observe is far away, seek Fox's aid as you imagine yourself close to that person or event, unseen as you watch what is going on from every angle.

AREAS TO EXPLORE

Fox's ability to blend into the landscape is an important part of its survival. It maintains a balance between retaining this invisibility and making his presence known. For many of us, however, blending in can become such a habit that not only do others cease to see us but we no longer see ourselves.

In early childhood, we often learn that it is not safe to make our needs known. We are taught not to express who we really are or to exercise those aspects of ourselves that make us unique. Instead, we observe carefully until we have discovered what others expect of us, and then we confine ourselves to what they wish us to do or be.

There are few people who do not suffer at least some discomfort from this learned invisibility. Mainly we feel the pain of not being appreciated for who we really are. With Fox as your support and guide, seek a deeper understanding of the ways in which you make yourself invisible. Seek a balance, using this skill to elude whomever you fear while knowing how to express the needs and abilities of the person you really are.

XIV. ARMADILLO

▲ *Variety in one's inner life*
▲ *Thick-skinned*
▲ *Nocturnal*
▲ *Ability to live in a narrow niche of its own*
▲ *Gentle, slow-moving, and reserved*

LEGEND

Armadillo's defense is to curl up in a ball, presenting only a tough-skinned exterior to the world. Animals who would prey on it thus cannot reach its soft, vulnerable underbelly. Because this slow-moving, nocturnal edentate (animal with no teeth) lives largely on insects such as ants, it presents little competition to other animals and thus goes mostly unnoticed by them.

By its nature and by its God-given physical attributes, Armadillo lives in a world almost completely unlike that of the animals assigned to guard the six regions. Although it is gentle and warm-blooded, it shares much with the reptiles, especially the tortoise. Being tooth-less, living on insects, and depending for their defense on their own thick armor, both creatures travel the desert floor on clumsy, short legs, ignored by most animals that might do them harm.

In Zuni folktales, Coyote is one of the few animals who ever goes to battle with Armadillo or seeks it out as a potential meal. But Armadillo outwits him each time, rolling itself into an impenetrable ball and sending Coyote into a quixotic frenzy that usually ends with him bruising his snout.

While not a traditional Zuni fetish figure, Armadillo figures have become quite popular. Many people feel drawn to Armadillo for its quiet reserve, its sense of invulnerability, and its attitude of comic detachment as it plods along, knowing that any animal with a grain of self-respect and with good reasoning capacities will give it a wide berth. Armadillo lives in its own little world, its physical characteristics, eating patterns, and general behavior clearly limiting its companions to those of its own kind.

Most people who include Armadillo among their fetishes do so not because of its powerful medicine but as a pet with qualities that are whimsical, endearing, and intriguing. On a deeper level, this animal may represent certain emotions or past experiences that we feel a need to isolate and protect in ourselves. All of us have such emotions and experiences, which are important to the overall integrity of our psyches. Even so, they are usually not key events in our lives. Because such emotions are not particularly significant, it is possible to keep them isolated and protected, sometimes forever. By turning to Armadillo, we pay homage to them without forcing them out into the light of day.

The millions of species who populate the world provide life with color and variety, filling every niche of the physical environment and maintaining the planet's homeostatic balance. So also there are great varieties of memories and emotions in our lives that all help to maintain a balance in the ecology of the mind. Armadillo reminds us that there is much in our inner world that is mysterious, that need not be explored, uncovered, or understood. There are memories that are minor elements in an alchemy whose purpose is to provide variety, color, and texture.

AFFIRMATIONS

Enrich your life by having Armadillo help you recall seemingly unimportant but happy or intriguing experiences from your past. Though such events may seem minor, together they are like the flecks of random color in a large beautiful weaving, whose beauty would be diminished if they were absent.

In sad moments or moments when you are lonely, focus on one or two minor past experiences when you felt complete and whole. Do not judge the memory or the original experience at all. Rather, curl up around it, like Armadillo curling up to protect its vulnerable belly; for the time being, turn your armored back to the world. Let yourself be comforted by simple pleasures.

AREAS TO EXPLORE

With Armadillo in your hand, let yourself be attentive to your response to this animal. What past experiences pop into your mind as you study this fetish and hold its image in your mind? What are your Armadillo thoughts and feelings? Honor the gentle, seemingly insignificant experiences of your life. Honor them as you would honor each of the infinite variety of plants, animals, minerals, earth, water, and air beings. Recognize that without this wondrous variety our earth would become barren and dull. Seek what seems unimportant in yourself, and elevate it with your gratitude.

XV. TURTLE

▲ *Symbol of the earth ("Turtle Island")*
▲ *Tenacity*
▲ *Self-reliance*
▲ *Nonviolent defense*
▲ *Skilled navigator*
▲ *Connection with the "center"*

LEGEND

Some animals defend themselves with sharp claws and teeth or with strength or speed. Turtle has none of these. Its defense is the hard shell that it carries with it everywhere, providing it with a roof over its head as well as protection from those who would do it harm.

Slow moving and clumsy, Turtle is greatly limited in the terrain over which it can travel, due to the size and bulk of its shell. It therefore chooses its journey with caution, plotting out a path ahead of time in order to minimize its use of energy and avoid getting into a place where it cannot move.

The age-old tale of the Tortoise and the Hare still describes this animal's demeanor; it is tenacious, sticking steadfastly to business, undaunted by distractions. Turtle gets the job done while other less mindful creatures procrastinate, putter, then fall far behind.

Perhaps most important of all, we should remember that to the Native Americans of most regions the earth is also known as "Turtle Island." In this way, the Turtle fetish represents the living spirit of Mother Earth herself. Interestingly, in recent research, astronomers exploring the edges of the universe have found that the known universe is shaped approximately like a turtle—slightly oval, with an outline like that of a flying saucer, thick in the middle, thin at the edges. Could it be that the ancient peoples had a way of seeing this, perhaps through the mind's eye, and they knew that it was not just Mother Earth but the universe itself that had this shape?

It is said that Turtle navigates, both on land and in the water, through its psychic connections with Mother Earth. Like Mole, Turtle is highly attuned to the energies of the earth and to what the Hopis refer to as the "cobwebs" that connect all things with all others. Through this network, Turtle communicates with Mother Earth. Thus, Turtle is an excellent messenger for carrying our prayers to the earth, while symbolically Turtle is the spirit of the living Earth herself.

AFFIRMATIONS

When you feel scattered or even lost, call upon Turtle to guide you. Put Turtle before you, or simply hold the image of this animal in your mind. Feel its centeredness, its perfect sense of direction, its confidence, its patience. If your thoughts are flying around in all directions, imagine Turtle sitting comfortably in the shade, solidly connected, as if by its own radar system, to the center of the earth. Imagine yourself to be Turtle, with all your thoughts settling down, gathering gently and easily under your shell. Feel confident that you need do nothing about any of the thoughts you are presently having. Release yourself from their "wind" and come into the silence of your Turtle mind, that part of you that is securely connected with the earth. When you once again feel centered, choose a single thought to respond to, knowing that you need do nothing more.

When you are feeling angry and hostile or you are being attacked, remind yourself of Turtle's way of dealing with potential threats. Its motto is "do no harm." It is not necessary to strike back or injure those whom we perceive as our enemies. There are many times when withdrawing into our shell is our best defense. Later, when the danger has passed, we may wish to seek help or take action that will prevent such attacks from taking place again.

AREAS TO EXPLORE

Most of us today have become disconnected from Mother Earth. Without this connection, we forget that she is the provider of all that nurtures our bodies. Just as the tiny baby learns that it must not bite the nipple of the breast that feeds it, so we must learn that we cannot injure our Mother without deep consequences.

Many modern troubles are the direct result of our disconnection from the earth. Poverty, illness, alienation from others and ourselves, loneliness, fear that we are without support or love—all these are symptoms of one illness: our disconnection from our true source. Explore how you might heal these symptoms in yourself by working with Turtle, asking this fetish how you might experience once again the peacefulness of this connection.

XVI. FROG

▲ *Our primordial cousin*
▲ *A reminder of common bonds with all of life*
▲ *Singer of songs that celebrate the most ancient watery beginnings*

LEGEND

Though not a traditional fetish, the figure of Frog appears in much Zuni artwork, such as on bowls or in weavings. Stories of Frog appear throughout the Native American literature, where it is often associated with the coming of rains to encourage the growth of crops.

Frog begins life in the water. It spends the first part of its life as a fish, swimming freely in ponds, lakes, rivers, and marshes. Then it slowly transforms, growing legs, losing its gills, developing the lungs of a land creature, losing its tail, then expanding the size of its head and mouth, until it is quite unlike its former self.

Since Frog is a very peculiar sort of being, with each individual member of its species repeating the evolution from swimmer to creature of the land, it can serve to remind us of our own development. We, too, begin as tiny, fishlike creatures, existing in an amniotic universe that echoes the great seas out of which life originally emerged on our planet.

Frog reminds us of the common bonds we humans share with all the creatures of this planet. The fish of the sea, the birds of the air, even the greatest of beasts begin as tiny swimmers; at this swimming stage, all species look very much alike. It is as if we have all come from a single egg, which in a very real sense we have, since we are all manifestations of a single life force.

If we listen carefully, the songs of Frog—whether the deep groaning of a giant bullfrog or the high-pitched chirping of the tiniest tree frog—can fill us with primordial stirrings. Their songs revive in us memories that are millions of years old yet still present in every life form.

AFFIRMATIONS

The planetary problems we are encountering today—everything from war and overpopulation to the deterioration of the ozone layer—have their roots in our feelings of separation from other creatures of the planet. We can injure our environment and other species only if we can learn to perceive ourselves as superior to them or as independent of them. This illusion of separation not only alienates us from the planet and its creatures but it also alienates us from ourselves. When this occurs we begin to experience feelings of loneliness, an inner longing that is difficult to identify or even acknowledge. We may feel that we are completely on our own, with no dependable support and help from any source. While there is no "quick fix" for reestablishing our common bond with all creatures of the planet, the Frog fetish can remind us of the watery beginnings we share; through Frog we can remember that we all come from the same life source.

Hold the image of Frog in your mind, along with all the images of its various life stages, from tiny swimmer, to tadpole, to Frog. Acknowledge the parallels in your own early development—from tiny swimmer to infant. Meditate on this evidence of our shared beginnings.

AREAS TO EXPLORE

With the Frog fetish before you or while holding it in your hand, first acknowledge the affirmation just described, then explore in your own mind the various ways you may deny the simple truth of our common bonds. Note how modern society has become numb to the presence of all but those household pets who have partially bridged the gap between species. Let Frog expand the awareness of your connection with all living things on the planet.

Whenever you hear the songs of frogs, think of them as celebrating the earliest beginnings of life on this plane, as well as our own emergence from Mother Earth's womb.

XVII. DEER (BISON)*

▲ *Ability to sacrifice for the higher good*
▲ *Moderation*
▲ *Understanding of what's necessary for survival*
▲ *Grace and appreciation for the beauty of balance*
▲ *Power of gratitude and giving*

LEGEND

In Zuni stories, the deer is a major resource for the community. These animals provided the people not only with food but with hides, bones, and antlers from which the Zunis made everything from garments to artwork, tools, and fetishes.

Many Zuni tales describe the deer in loving and reverent terms. The Zunis looked upon the deer as a gift of the gods, providing them with many of their basic needs. For this reason, they were careful,

---

* What Deer was to the people of the desert, Bison was to the plains people farther north. Many legends, such as the one recorded here, were interchangeable for Bison and Deer. Since there is little evidence that the Zuni ever hunted the bison, fetishes of them found in early Zuni suggest that they made them for plains people to the north.

before killing such an animal, to express their gratitude and pray for its soul that it might, after death, take form once again.

There is one story about a child who is adopted by the Deer people. He is the offspring of a union between a beautiful young Zuni woman and Father Sun. The young woman, wanting to hide her pregnancy from her father, takes her newborn out into the mountains and leaves him there; he is adopted by the Deer people.

The boy is taught the ways of the Deer and grows up to be very strong, eating as the deer eat and living as they live. One day a hunter from his mother's community sees the boy with the deer and takes this news back to his village. The hunters band together to go after the herd of deer and attempt to capture the boy himself.

The boy wants to protect the Deer people, whom he loves because they are his adopted family. But the deer reply that they are accustomed to being hunted. They explain that they do not mind because there are many hunters who are sacred of heart and sacred of thought among the boy's original people. These hunters make sacrifices to the deer, ensuring that their spiritual forms are spared and thus that they are given immortal life.

The deer implore the boy to allow the hunters to pursue and kill them. He is then to go back to his village and become one of his mother's people again. Once this is accomplished, he is to educate other hunters about the Deer and about the proper ways of hunting them.

The hunters come, make their sacrifices and prayers, and the deer willingly offer themselves up to be killed, sacrificing their flesh to the hunters and their families. The hunters capture the boy, who is brought back to the town. Following his mother's confession of how she had abandoned the boy when he was still a baby, she gives penance, is forgiven, and is thus reunited with her son.

The boy becomes a great hunter. With his extensive wisdom of the Deer, he is much sought after by other hunters. He imparts his knowledge of the Deer and their ways willingly and instructs other hunters in the sacred rituals of offering gratitude, sacrifices, and prayers for the immortality of the Deer. He has no regrets about giving this information because he understands that the Deer willingly offer their flesh to the people, knowing it will be received in a sacred way.

The relationship between people and the Deer that the Ashiwi understood expresses their deep understanding and appreciation for the spiritual links between all beings. In the stories told about Deer, we see the importance of honoring the spirit of all beings and of perceiving that our lives cannot be explained only in terms of our physical selves.

Also in the stories of Deer, there is an understanding of the need to conserve the resources we have been given. To use resources unwisely, greedily, or selfishly can mean that they will one day run out. Again and again, the sacred path of the traditional Ashiwi hunter is defined as one where these principles are honored. They who use more than they need are punished, usually by the deities, while those who honor the sacred ways are rewarded with a good and comfortable life.

AFFIRMATIONS

When a relationship gets out of balance, as most do from time to time, with one person seeming to give much more than the other, place the Deer fetish before you. Ask yourself where you are feeling the most imbalance: are you giving too much and thus feeling that you are carrying the burden of responsibility in this relationship? Or is the other person giving so much that you feel uncomfortable— manipulated or controlled by him or her through that person's apparent generosity? Let Deer remind you that balance in giving and receiving is the key to a happy relationship. There are many ways to keep this balance: by giving to each other more or less equally, by expressing gratitude to the giver, and by receiving what is given with joy.

When you are feeling short of resources, deprived emotionally, materially, or spiritually, place the Deer fetish before you and contemplate its meanings and messages. One of the key principles that we find in the Deer stories is the importance of gratitude. When we offer gratitude, we are following a sacred instruction, and this simple act can be empowering, lifting our spirits. To offer gratitude sincerely—even at those times when we find ourselves wanting to focus on what we lack—renews our energy, our hope, and our trust in powers greater than ourselves. With gratitude given purely, we open ourselves to receiving.

AREAS TO EXPLORE

Deer is a reminder that giving and receiving are the same. If you are feeling that you are giving too much, explore your expectations. What do you wish to get in return? Are you expecting a reward? Are you doing penance? Do you feel that you are valued by others only through your giving? Most of us will find one or all of these things are true, or at least partially true, about us. Once we acknowledge these feelings, we can choose to free ourselves of such hidden agendas. To give purely—with no strings attached—is its own immediate pleasure and reward.

Similarly, to receive we must begin with gratitude, offering prayers of thanksgiving for what we now have and for what we have been given in the past. Through gratitude we begin to discover one of the great spiritual truths—that what we get from life is not the result of our own isolated efforts but is the outcome of a complex synergy between ourselves and everything around us. Let the Deer fetish guide you to this realization.

XVIII. HORSE

▲ *Power*
▲ *Expanding one's own potential abilities*
▲ *Control of the environment*
▲ *Interspecies communication*
▲ *Awareness of power achieved with true cooperation*

LEGEND

Although not a traditional Zuni fetish, figures of horses made by Zuni carvers have been popular among other tribes for perhaps hundreds of years. Today they are still carved by the Zunis and are collected by people of all backgrounds.

Throughout history, the horse has played a significant role in humanity's evolution and has been immortalized in everything from Greek mythology to Hollywood films. The horse represents the power of the animal world literally "harnessed" for the benefit of the human race.

From the moment they first climbed on the backs of horses, humans were transformed. They experienced dominance over creatures larger than themselves. They experienced speed and the ability to travel great distances in a short period of time without tiring. They gained the ability to run down game animals, such as the buffalo or deer, which they could not do on foot.

Horses gave people the ability to cultivate vast portions of the earth and to carry burdens over distances that could otherwise never have been covered. On the simplest practical level, the benefits derived from domesticating the horse in these ways were indeed great. In a broader sense, they symbolize the human's effort to control nature and in this way be less at the mercy of the natural environment.

The experience of being astride a horse changed humanity's perception of itself. In that single act, we suddenly commanded the power of an animal much larger and infinitely more powerful physically than ourselves. In this way we expanded our own capacities and our own view of ourselves, suddenly perceiving the world in new ways. It is no wonder that prior to the internal combustion engine, many nations the world over measured their power according to how many horses they owned.

The literature of nearly every nation is filled with stories about the special relationships established between horses and humans. Indeed, the mythological centaur, half horse and half man, symbolizes the actual merging of the two into a single form.

People who work with horses or who enjoy them for recreation know of the close communication that can be established between animal and human. Whether one is racing, cutting cattle, or just out for a leisurely ride, there are many moments that would not be half so exciting or gratifying if these two separate species had not learned to share common goals and pleasures.

Although it is undoubtedly overplayed in popular literature, there is considerable evidence that horses are able to develop strong emotional attachments to their owners. Like dogs and cats, they seem to desire and require expressions of affection from the humans in their lives. They can be playful and even mischievous, suggesting that the bond established between our two species has a spiritual component that extends beyond the human being's compulsion to exploit other creatures.

AFFIRMATIONS

When you are feeling powerless, place the Horse before you or hold an image of it in your mind. The strength you feel as you contemplate the Horse may be evoked by your experience of its power and speed in real life. But you could neither feel nor in any way experience that power unless it was a potential within yourself. If you do not immediately feel anything, stick with it, letting the Horse figure remind you of every horse you have ever seen. Hold the image of the Horse and its power in your mind, and let these feelings spread throughout your entire being.

When struggling with issues of control or dominance, place the Horse before you. Remember that the skillful horseperson is one who is constantly weighing whether to exert or surrender control—in essence, the rider is constantly deciding when to trust the animal's judgment and when to trust his or her own. Thus, the most pleasurable and productive relationships are cooperative ones, where all participants respect the power of others and make room for it without relinquishing their own power.

Mere dominance over others—that is, control for the sake of control—may temporarily get us what we think we want, but it does not provide us with the full benefit of the other's power. We can get the latter only through respect of that power and a willingness to allow it to blossom. This requires some risk and a willingness to surrender our fears about losing control.

Holding the image of Horse in your mind keeps you centered on the fact that the only real power is not power over the actions of others or over nature but the power to make your own decisions, to choose how you think, feel, and act. To keep your relationships happy and productive, whether at work, at home, or at play, you need to make certain that you give both yourself and others equal space to exercise this power. Thus, the word *cooperation* suggests a way of working together that allows everyone involved to operate at his or her highest potential, both in terms of what is produced and in terms of the satisfaction each person receives.

AREAS TO EXPLORE

The Horse naturally evokes both positive and negative images for most people. On the one hand, we are reminded of humanity's drive and relative success in gaining certain limited control over the environment. On the other hand, we are reminded that many of the ways in which we have accomplished this have been harmful. We may, for example, develop poisons to destroy insect pests that threaten our crops, but in the process we may also pollute the sources far beneath the soil from which we draw our drinking water. We may clear the Brazilian rain forest to make room for vast ranches and farms but in the process threaten the ozone layer that protects us from the harmful rays of the sun.

The relationship we have established with the horse suggests that dominance over nature or over others does not gain us real power in the long run. It only diminishes the potential power of what we attempt to control. The beauty we enjoy in horse and rider comes from experiencing the power of two species working together with respect for each other's unique contributions.

To explore these same concepts in all our relationships is just one of the values of the Horse fetish. Wherever there is conflict, wherever love seems to be temporarily lost, seek Horse's assistance in reminding you of the importance of respecting each other's power.

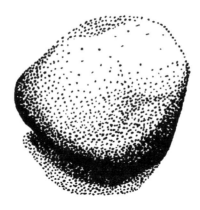

XIX. MIRROR STONE

▲ *Self-knowledge*
▲ *Transformation and healing*

LEGEND

Although not a traditional Zuni fetish, the Mirror Stone is one that I began working with several years ago. The idea is to choose as your fetish a stone that has no particular distinguishing features. It should look like nothing more than what it is, a stone. As such, you can let it be anything you wish, knowing that any identity you assign to it is a product of your own mind. This is the reason it is called Mirror Stone, because whatever we see in it is a reflection of our own thoughts and feelings.

How then can this fetish be useful to us? I place it before me, either alone or within a fetish consulting circle, and allow it to stand for any difficulties I am having in my own life. If I am having a problem with another person, I allow the stone to be that person. If I am having difficulty with an object or situation, I allow it to be that object or situation. Then I begin an inner monologue with it: "I cannot work with this person anymore. This person is too critical of others, including me. This person has a very negative outlook on life . . ." or whatever comes bubbling up in my mind at that moment.

As you experiment with this process, let the monologue flow. When you get to a stopping point, pause and meditate on the stone as your mirror. Tell yourself, "I alone am responsible for all that I have said and felt here. I have made all this in my mind." Do this even though you may feel totally justified about the thoughts and feelings that the other person or the situation has provoked in you. Focus now only on the fact that what you have just expressed is of your own making.

Let the Mirror Stone contain all this. Be silent and ask for it to speak to you. You may ask it whatever questions you wish. I like to ask, "If you were a wise and gentle teacher, how would you verbally express the lesson you would have me learn from this difficult person or situation?" Another question might be "In what ways are my thoughts and feelings benefiting me or hurting me? If the latter, how can I let them go?"

Because we get into the habit of looking upon what we feel as being caused by outside forces, it usually takes practice to get into working with the Mirror Stone. Also, we have a great resistance to thinking about ourselves in this way. However, to see that *we* make our own thoughts and feelings, that they are not made by people or situations outside us, is tremendously empowering. As a practice for learning self-power, any work you do with the Mirror Stone will be tremendously rewarding.

AFFIRMATIONS

When you are feeling powerless or victimized by a person or situation that seems beyond your control, place the Mirror Stone before you. Express the dark feelings you are experiencing and let the stone become those feelings. Remind yourself that regardless of the situation, you are the maker of these feelings. Whether you can completely believe this or not, let it be true for this moment.

As a maker of feelings, take a moment to recognize your power. Note the effect of what you have made on your body—muscular tensions, the side effects of frustration and rage (increased heart rate) or depression (shallow breathing). You might also note how these same feelings affect people around you, triggering their fear, their concern for you, or their anger. All this represents a great amount of energy, some held within your own body, some moving outside you.

In terms of raw energy, *all that you make* is a potential power. And all of this is personal power, energy available to you to use as you choose.

Let fetishes other than the Mirror Stone help you with your personal power. For example, to set the limits of how your energy will be used, turn to Mountain Lion; to discover when to draw back inside yourself and gather your energy, look to Bear; to decide when to use your energy aggressively, consult with Badger.

When you are feeling numb or without emotion, use the Mirror Stone. Many times, in the face of a personal crisis, when confronted with a great loss, or when we find ourselves in double-bind situations where it appears that anything we might do will be wrong, we simply go numb. There's a sensation that we have no thoughts or emotions at all.

Of course, we never really lose our ability to think and feel. We only turn off those abilities when life becomes too difficult. The Mirror Stone can help us turn these powers on again. To do so, place the stone before you and begin your monologue with a statement of exactly what you are experiencing at that moment: "I am feeling nothing but numbness . . ." The goal is simply to focus on the present entirely, describing whatever is on your mind right now, even if it is nothing. You will open up slowly or rapidly—the speed at which you do so is dictated by your own readiness to participate actively in your life again.

AREAS TO EXPLORE

In working with the Mirror Stone, take time to explore the stone itself. Of what material is it made, for example? What do we know of the origins of this material? In any material that comes from Mother

Earth, we generally have an ageless collection of history, with elemental particles dating back to the beginning of matter and energy. What stories, then, does this stone contain? Questions such as these can take us to the outer limits of our capacity to know; according to many of the elders, this is where true wisdom begins.

As you confront the limits of your knowledge, you will begin to recognize the stone's own mystery. There is much more that we cannot know of this simple object than we can know of it. Let this remind you that we cannot know all that is in another person's mind; most of what we know is only the product of our own minds. The same is true of any situation. The only truth we can really be sure of is that what we think we know is of our own making. Our perception may or may not connect with greater truths or greater powers.

Preface

1. Mary Austen, Introduction, in Frank Hamilton Cushing, *Zuni Folk Tales* (Tucson: University of Arizona Press, 1988), xxi.

2. Austen, in Cushing, *Zuni Folk Tales*, xxiii.

3. Austen, in Cushing, *Zuni Folk Tales*, xxix.

Introduction

1. As quoted by Joseph Campbell during a workshop at Esalen Institute, Big Sur, California, 1984.

2. Albert Einstein, "What I Believe," in *Out of My Later Years* (London: Thames & Hudson, 1950), 123.

Chapter One

1. Tom Bahti, Introduction, in Frank Hamilton Cushing, *Zuni Fetishes*, facsimile ed. (Las Vegas, NV: KC Publications, 1974), n.p.

2. Frank Hamilton Cushing, *Zuni Breadstuff: Indian Notes and Monographs* (New York: Museum of the American Indian Heye Foundation, 1920), 422–423.

3. Cushing, *Zuni Breadstuff*, 91–92.

4. Frank Hamilton Cushing, "Outlines of Zuni Creation Myths," Thirteenth Annual Report to the Bureau of American Ethnology (Washington, D.C.: Bureau of American Ethnology, 1896), 380.

5. Ralph Waldo Emerson, "Compensation," in *Essays: First and Second Series* (Boston: Houghton, 1883), 353.

6. Some anthropologists have gone so far as to suggest that the Zunis may actually be one of the "lost tribes of Israel," though others have disputed this claim.

7. Cushing, *Zuni Fetishes*, 41.

8. Extrapolated from Cushing, *Zuni Fetishes*.

9. Ruth F. Kirk, *Zuni Fetishism* (Albuquerque, NM: Avanyu Publishing, 1988), 32.

10. Kirk, *Zuni Fetishism*, 67.

11. Kirk, *Zuni Fetishism*, 121.

12. Cushing, *Zuni Fetishes*, 31.

13. Cushing, *Zuni Fetishes*, 38.

Chapter Two

1. Nancy Wood, *Many Winters* (New York: Doubleday, 1974), 57.

2. The prey fetishes of the hunt are usually the same as the fetishes of the six regions, with the exception of Coyote, which replaces Black Bear in the west, and Wildcat, which replaces Badger in the south. There are numerous variations on these designations, determined in part by tradition and in part by the individual who owns the fetishes.

3. Austen, in Cushing, *Zuni Folk Tales*, xxii.

4. Lao Tzu, *The Way of Lao Tzu*, trans. Wing-Tsit Chan (Indianapolis: Bobbs-Merrill, 1963), 14.

5. Mircea Eliade, *Essential Sacred Writings from Around the World* (San Francisco: Harper & Row, 1977), 572.

6. Eliade, *Essential Sacred Writings*, 572.

Chapter Three

1. Cushing, *Zuni Fetishes*, 11.

Chapter Four

1. Cushing, "The Trial of Lovers," in *Zuni Folk Tales*, 1–33.

BIBLIOGRAPHY

Benedict, Ruth. *Zuni Mythology*. New York: Columbia University Press, 1935.

Bunzel, Ruth. *Zuni Katchinas: An Analytical Study*. Forty-Seventh Annual Report of the Bureau of American Ethnology. Washington, D.C.: Bureau of American Ethnology, 1929–1930.

———. *Zuni Texts*. American Ethnological Society Publications, vol. 15. New York: American Ethnological Society, 1933.

Castaneda, Carlos. *Journey to Ixtlan: The Lessons of Don Juan*. New York: Simon & Schuster, 1972.

Cushing, Frank Hamilton. *Zuni Breadstuff: Indian Notes and Monographs*. New York: Museum of the American Indian Heye Foundation, 1920.

———. *Zuni Fetishes*. Second Annual Report of the Bureau of American Ethnology. Washington, D.C.: Bureau of American Ethnology, 1883. Facsimile ed. Las Vegas, NV: KC Publications, 1974.

———. *Zuni Folk Tales*. Tucson: University of Arizona Press, 1988.

Eggan, Fred, and Eggan, Pandey. "Zuni History, 1855–1970." In Alfonso Ortiz (ed.), *Handbook of the North American Indian*, vol. 9. Washington, D.C.: Smithsonian Institution, 1973.

Eliade, Mircea. *Essential Sacred Writings from Around the World*. San Francisco: Harper & Row, 1977.

Erdoes, Richard. *Crying for a Dream*. Santa Fe, NM: Bear & Company, 1990.

Kirk, Ruth F. *Zuni Fetishism*. Albuquerque, NM: Avanyu Publishing, 1988.

Parsons, Elsie Clews. "Notes on Zuni." In *Memoirs*, vol. 4, no. 4, part 2. Lancaster, PA: American Anthropological Association, 1917.

Rodee, Marian, and Ostler, James. *Zuni Pottery*. West Chester, PA: Schiffer Publishing, 1986.

————. *The Fetish Carvers of Zuni*. Albuquerque: Maxwell Museum of Anthropology, University of New Mexico; and Zuni, NM: Pueblo of Zuni Arts and Crafts, 1990.

Sams, Jamie, and Carson, David. *Medicine Cards: The Discovery of Power Through the Ways of Animals*. Santa Fe, NM: Bear & Company, 1988.

Tedlock, Dennis (trans.). "Performances in the Zuni by Andrew Peynetsa and Walter Sanchez." In *Finding the Center: Narrative Poetry of the Zuni Indians*. Lincoln: University of Nebraska Press, 1972.

Vecsey, Christopher. *Imagine Ourselves Richly: Mythic Narratives of North American Indians*. San Francisco: HarperCollins, 1991.

Vroman, A. C. *Dwellers at the Source: Southwestern Indian Photographs of A. C. Vroman, 1895–1904*. Albuquerque: University of New Mexico Press, 1973.

Wasson, R. Gordon; Kramrisch, Stella; Ott, Jonathan; and Ruck, Carl A. P. *Persephone's Quest: Entheogens and the Origins of Religion*. New Haven, CT: Yale University Press, 1986.

Wood, Nancy. *Many Winters*. New York: Doubleday, 1974.

Wright, Barton (as written by Frank Hamilton Cushing, edited and illustrated by Barton Wright). *The Mythic World of the Zuni*. Albuquerque: University of New Mexico Press, 1988.

RESOURCES

There are many retailers throughout the United States that sell fetishes and other native crafts and art objects. The following is a list of some that I am aware of. Fetishes are also available in most museum gift shops.

Because fetishes are individually carved, with each one a little different, touching, feeling, and looking are the best ways to pick them out. However, if you live in a remote area where they are not readily available, Tony Barnett, at Southwest Indian Art, will work with you over the phone and supply you with what you need by mailorder.

Note that the first three retailers listed here are tribally owned galleries of the Zuni people.

Pueblo of Zuni Arts and Crafts
Milford Nahohai, Assistant Manager
P.O. Box 425
Zuni, NM 87327
(505) 782–5531

Zuni Pueblo
A Tribally Owned Gallery
Susan Allen, Manager
1749 Union Street
San Francisco, CA 94123
(415) 567–0941

Zuni Pueblo
A Tribally Owned Gallery
Bradley Allan, Manager
222–A Main Street
Venice, CA 90291
(310) 399–7792

Dandelion
Beth Fluke, Manager
1718 Sansom Street
Philadelphia, PA 19103
(215) 972–0999

KESHI
Santa Fe Village
Robin B. Dunlap, Manager
227 Don Gaspar Avenue
Santa Fe, NM 87501
(505) 989–8728

Nature Company
Outlets in many cities throughout the U.S. and overseas. Check phone book in your area or call for information at their corporate office in Berkeley, California
(800) 227–1114

Pacific Western Traders
Herb and Peggy Puffer, Managers
P. O. Box 95
305 Wool Streeet
Folsom, CA 95630
(916) 985–3851

Southwest Indian Art
Tony Barnett, Manager
P. O. Box 117
San Anselmo, CA 94960
(707) 645–8170